RAJI CUISINE

Indian Flavors, French Passion

Raji Jallepalli, with Judith Choate

Photography by Gozen Koshida and Steven Needham

Wine Notes by Shields Hood

HarperCollinsPublishers

RAJI CUISINE. Copyright © 2000 by Raji Jallepalli. All rights reserved. Printed in China. No part of this book may be used or reproduced in any manner whatsoever without written permission except in the case of brief quotations embodied in critical articles and reviews. For information address HarperCollins Publishers Inc., 10 East 53rd Street, New York, NY 10022.

HarperCollins books may be purchased for educational, business, or sales promotional use. For information please write: Special Markets Department, HarperCollins Publishers Inc., 10 East 53rd Street, New York, NY 10022.

FIRST EDITION

Designed by Ph.D

Photographs on the front and back cover and pages xii, 6, 11, 20, 21, 22, 23, 27, 31, 37, 42, 47, 51, 57, 65, 69, 72, 75, 99, 107, 117, 134, 137, 141, 149, 159, 165, 179, 197, and 205 by Gozen Koshida

Photographs on pages 54, 58, 79, 85, 91, 121, 125, 145, 167, 173, 175, 189, 193, 201, and 203 by Steven Needham

Library of Congress Cataloging-in-Publication Data

Jallepalli, Raji.

    Raji Cuisine: Indian flavors, French passion/Raji Jallepalli.—1st ed.

        cm.

    ISBN 0-06-019222-4

    1. Cookery, India. 2. Cookery, French. I. Title.

    TX74.5.I4J33 2000   99-16767

    641.5954—dc21

00 01 02 03 04 ❖/RRD 10 9 8 7 6 5 4 3 2 1

To my children, Prasad and Satish and Jen, with love, respect, and adoration,

and to Lou, my sweetheart, with all my love

Contents

Talking About Raji, by Charlie Trotter

Cuisine labeled as "fusion" more often than not has a negative connotation, the results frequently muddled or contrived. This is not the case, though, in the hands of Raji Jallepalli. Not only is she deeply knowledgeable about the flavors of her native Indian cuisine, but I swear she must have been a French aristocrat in a previous life! Her profound understanding of nuance and subtlety leads me to believe that she is well versed in the pleasures of French haute cuisine. Yet her food has a vitality and a glorious, assertive edge that trumpets her Indian heritage. Most startling, however, about her complex flavors and combinations, is the relative ease with which they can be put together. This is the truest sign of a great chef: minimalist approach, maximalist result!

I've heard some people call Raji the Spice Goddess, or Spice Queen, but I don't think those titles begin to do her justice. She doesn't just *use* spices; rather, their presence in her cuisine is an utterly intuitive expression. Raji is more like a Spice Poet with her use of cilantro, cinnamon, saffron, turmeric, ginger, cumin, and cardamom (among others), evidencing themselves with a lyricism, even a femininity, not with rugged, bold strokes. Yet the flavors and combinations are decidedly *there.*

The blending of French and Indian cuisine in her hands floats like notes from the late Yehudi Menuhin's violin. Hers becomes one cuisine—not a melding of two. It is completely natural; there is nothing contrived about it.

Another special quality of Raji's approach is her unbridled enthusiasm. You see, she came to her life as a chef later than most (indeed, after a successful career in medicine!), so her energy and passion still sizzle. In fact, the exuberance is translated right to the plate.

It excites me to know that we now have a collection of Raji's dishes in the written form. I'm certain I'll be "lifting" a few ideas from these pages for my own cuisine. After all—what are friends for?

Acknowledgments

Along this culinary big dipper, there are stars who must be acknowledged, as they have inspired me in a way no one else has.

Charlie Trotter, who invented tireless perfection with his incredible balance of passion for food and friendship. I feel very fortunate to be his friend and to have the opportunity to continue to learn from him. I have had so many memorable moments with Charlie and his wife, Lynn—in their home as well as guest cooking with Charlie, Emeril Lagasse, and Norman Van Aken.

Jean-Louis Palladin, who is quite simply the gold standard for my culinary life. His passion for cooking is intoxicating—watching him work in the kitchen has been truly inspiring for me. I cherish my friendship with Jean-Louis.

Michel Richard, who has cooked some memorable "art on the plate" meals for me. His sense of humor is extremely entertaining.

Shields Hood and I go back quite a long way. When I first opened my restaurant, he was there teaching me all that he knew about wines. Originally from Mississippi, Shields has a soft, slow accent that is an amusing counterpoint to his intensity about wine.

Alice Waters, whom I just recently had the opportunity to meet for the first time and whose knowledge and passion blew me away. I am in awe of all that she has done for American cuisine. I want to learn more from her!

I have been so fortunate to have Janis Donnaud as both my friend and my literary agent. She has been a delight to work with, and her help and support have been invaluable to me. Her initial belief in my ability to create a cookbook was really the impetus I needed to start the project. I really do owe her my most sincere thanks for believing in me and for always being there when I needed her.

Once the idea of a book was planted, I found Judie Choate to help me bring my voice to the printed page. Her knowledge of language, her appreciation of food, her gentleness and professionalism in urging me to put my vision into words joined together to make creating a cookbook easy for me. I will always be grateful for her help.

Before meeting Susan Friedland, my editor at HarperCollins, whose reputation as the finest cookbook editor is larger than life, I was terribly intimidated. Her immediate support made me feel that I was up to the job of putting Restaurant Raji between the covers of a book. It is her fine hand that has made the book live up to my expectations. Thank you, Susan.

These people all helped me show that I simply love to cook. Throughout the writing of my cookbook, I always felt their power telling me that I was not doing it alone. I will treasure this experience for the rest of my life.

Introduction

Before you ask, let me tell you that I don't know how I came to open a restaurant in Memphis, Tennessee. Oh, I can tell you the specifics of time, place, and budget, but I really can't pinpoint the moment when I knew that everything about my life was changing. Cooking was taking the place of a medical career, pushing me farther away from the traditional role of wife and mother. Perhaps the only answer is kismet; even as I was standing in the laboratory, incubating tissue, fate had framed my future, and it was not under my control at all. It is as good an answer as any I have been able to formulate.

When I was a child in the city of Hyderabad in South India, I would often sneak into the kitchen to bother the cook with nagging questions about whatever happened to be on the stove. My parents, trying very hard to school me in the proper behavior of a lady, did not encourage my attempts at domesticity. Indian ladies did not cook; there was no imaginable reason for me to waste my (and Cook's) time in the kitchen. Nevertheless, I persevered. The artistry of the kitchen appealed to me as much as the alchemy. It would just take me many years to recognize that the science and art of the culinary world were much more satisfying to me than was the well-ordered laboratory of a microbiologist who happened to also love the fine arts.

Throughout my life, I have been blessed with experiences that have encouraged adventure. My father was a diplomat who exposed his family to the cultures of the world. Although we had a very traditional and conservative household, my father was a staunch advocate of education, even for women. He felt it was important that his daughters be prepared for an integrated world community. Medicine became, for me, the road to that community. I never once considered the time-honored stay-at-home role expected of an Indian woman. But even so, I did marry an Indian physician and have two sons as I was building my career in the lab.

When my husband's growing medical practice demanded it, I became his office manager, discovering that the precision required in the laboratory served me well as I organized and ran his business. I now see how all of these careers—microbiologist, wife, mother, office manager—would come together and enable me to find the stamina and skill to become the chef-owner of a restaurant.

Restaurant Raji, where I practice my own, very personal excursion into fusion cooking, began in 1989 as the East Indian Trading Company, serving traditional Indian food. Although I considered myself a Francophile, traveling to France frequently to indulge my love of classic French foods and wines, I never gave a thought to including French cuisine or wine on my menu. In France in the early eighties, I do remember thinking, This food could use some of the assertive flavors of my homeland as well as some lightening up. These thoughts must have stayed with me, since once I gained some confidence at the stove, I plunged into experimentation, integrating the flavors and techniques of classic Indian cooking with the principles and techniques of the haute cuisine of my beloved France. As I became bolder, I used the spirit of California light-ness to conceive menus that are bursting with flavor yet delicate, healthful yet complex, and naturally low in fat but exceptionally satisfying. And somehow in Memphis, the land of barbecue, the concept of French-Indian fusion cuisine was born.

More often than not, I am asked, "Just what is fusion cuisine?" I find that French-Indian fusion often elicits, "Foie gras and curry? No way!" Well, it isn't foie gras and curry—although subtly done, I guarantee that the combination would work—but it is a rather quiet melding of vastly different cultures, philosophies, and cooking techniques. While mastering the art of French cooking, one learns to embrace the finesse, formality, control, and order of the classic restaurant cuisine that has evolved primarily through the hands of male chefs. In Indian cooking, you will find simple and quite ancient kitchen traditions laced with spontaneity, intense bouquets, and a very basic approach to preparing inviting meals that has evolved through the hands of women in the home kitchen. Using very simple ingredients, such as potatoes or tomatoes, prepared in the style of each cuisine, you would find that the French dish would result in a sublime expression of the precise flavor of the main ingredient, while the Indian one would give you an intense explosion of a combination of heat and spice that would almost overpower the main ingredient. In my kitchen, for the most part, I retain the basic principles and balance of French cuisine while introducing the profound bouquets of Indian cooking.

As it has matured, my approach to fusion cooking has become a style in and of itself. It has its distinctive and quite personal body and soul evolving from technique, heritage, and knowledge. When planning a menu, I begin in the marketplace, choosing only the freshest ingredients available on any given day. I then think of the texture, color, flavor, and lightness that I want to create on the plate. To do this, I rely on the deeply sensual memories provoked by culinary experiences from my past. For I believe, once you have tasted something, the aroma, texture, and essence are yours to recapture and reformulate. If you learn to trust your memory bank of flavors and tastes as you visualize your menu, what you mentally envision and what actually happens on the plate will be very close to one another.

None of this is complicated. I am totally self-taught in the kitchen, which I think allows me the freedom to venture into areas trained chefs would be reluctant to follow. Having never been schooled in the rules of the culinary workplace, I am unaware of those that can't be broken. Therefore, I have nothing to confine or restrict my creativity. I use my intellect to examine the principles of cooking. I depend upon my curiosity to help me consider the whys of cooking. And when something doesn't work, I don't allow failure to intimidate me. Rather, I let it serve as the catalyst for more research and development.

All of the recipes in this book come from my restaurant kitchen, where I work alone, with only one assistant to help scrub, peel, and clean up my mess. I plan each plate so that all of the components will come together easily at service time. Since I don't have heat lamps, every dish has to speed from my stove to the table just as it must in a home kitchen. I think that all of these considerations will allow my recipes to be easily re-created in your kitchen. Writing down recipes is a necessary evil, but, it will please me if you think of these recipes as rough sketches for your own culinary adventure, and use your own memory bank as the guiding light to create restaurant-style dining in your own home.

Don't think of cooking as a competition. It should be an inspiration. If you set out to impress your guests, you will always find yourself falling short. It doesn't work in our social lives, and it certainly doesn't work at mealtime. Learn to enjoy your time in the kitchen by having faith in your unique individuality. Composing a meal under duress will only bring chaos to the table. I am sure that you will find as I have that finer meals are created when you are candid, relaxed, and trusting of your creativity.

When I first opened Restaurant Raji, I thought that I would have to be a tyrant, just as I imagined the great French chefs to be. I learned, through some difficult times, that serenity and grace serve me—and the restaurant diners—in a much better fashion. My patrons come into the restaurant to get away from the everyday world. It is my goal to meet them with kindness and consideration, surround them with harmony, and then provide a tremendous dining experience, always accompanied by great wines. I have found that when embraced by serenity, even the most challenging critic will excuse the imperfections that are, from time to time, unavoidable.

When dining at Restaurant Raji, many people feel as though they have been entertained in my home. For me, this is a major accomplishment. I do not have a "homey" restaurant but I have worked very hard to create a formal yet welcoming space. In my generation, women chefs are comfortable enough in the profession to draw inspiration from their femininity without relying on girlishness or being cute. I like to think that this is one of the reasons for my success. In medicine, in the kitchen and the restaurant, and throughout my life I have looked for the same thing: the perfect salt-to-sugar balance.

One of the most joyful and sociable ingredients of my adventures in the restaurant trade has been my growing understanding of how fine wines complete a meal. Now I often prepare complex meals for wine collectors. It is terribly exciting to match my menus to wines that challenge me to be as creative as I can. As I devise a menu, the wines that I will offer with each course are uppermost in my mind. It is always stimulating to choose all the right ingredients to complement the fine nuances that great wines offer. When used with a discriminating hand, spices seem to dance with heady wines of the Rhône or the complex vintages of Bordeaux. In the restaurant, I have only a small wine list as it takes some time, and a great deal of money, to build a wine cellar. But if a wine that is not on my list will best complement my menu, I will order it for the occasion and advertise it as a special event.

With the good counsel of my friend, colleague, and wine expert extraordinaire, Shields Hood, I have suggested wines to serve with the recipes in this book. I hope that our recommendations will introduce you to the satisfaction that good wines can induce and the passion that great wines can provoke. I can't imagine dining without a glass of wine at my plate, and I hope that I can lead you to the same intense feelings about the grape.

As you read through my recipes and menus, sharing my good fortune in the generosity and wisdom of valued friends and superb chefs, the extravagance of the great wines of the world, and the abundance of my life, think of me as your own special genie. When you lift the lids off the jars of spices to which I have introduced you, I want you to feel a bit of my spirit urging you on to discover your own personal style of cooking. Use my recipes, but don't allow them to restrict your imagination. Trust yourself and you, like me, might wake up one day with your wildest fantasy a reality. It really has been an incredible journey.

Raji's Pantry

My restaurant guests frequently ask to take a tour of my kitchen. They are always quite surprised to find a small, compact space in which I seem to be getting ready to feed a large family, rather than restaurant diners. They find that my fusion pantry is filled with all of the usual fresh and fine-quality ingredients found in many restaurant kitchens, along with some Indian specialties that are part and parcel of any Indian home kitchen. None of the ingredients that I use are difficult to find, and most of them have readily available substitutes.

Since my kitchen is small, I keep my supplies well organized, with a lovely array of spices, rices and grains, oils, and a variety of lentils always on hand. Frozen phyllo and other pastry doughs are at the ready for last-minute inspirations. Fresh brown eggs, wonderful cheeses, and perfume-filled fresh herbs are always in the refrigerator. Other perishables are ordered daily; fresh pastas and breads, fish and shellfish, caviars, foie gras, meats (both commonplace and exotic), and organic fruits and vegetables are brought to my kitchen door within hours of being ordered. Express shipping allows me to find a garden, field, and stream at my back door every day. Even when those demanding gourmets from all over the world drop by, unannounced, requesting fourteen courses of a spontaneous degustation (tasting) menu, I can work my own miracles with little effort, thanks to everything I have on hand.

You will find that I use onions more frequently than the shallots most often called for in French cooking, as I find that shallots impart a sharp taste when combined with spices. I use all the fresh herbs of classic French cuisine as well as a great deal of cilantro (I particularly love cilantro!) and fresh hot chiles, identified with traditional Indian cooking. I try to balance the flavors so that a gentle melding of cultures is experienced on the palate.

Far more than any other ingredient or technique, the ingenious use of spices and seasonings distinguishes Indian cooking from all other cuisines. By using spices and herbs in their various guises—whole, ground, roasted, fried, dried, or fresh—the cook can elicit a broad spectrum of flavors that, in turn, can season simple dishes in ever-changing ways. When cooking with spices, think first of the texture, flavor, and color of the main ingredient of the recipe and then imagine the palette of seasonings that you will want to overlay and meld into it. Once you master the use of spices and the classic Indian techniques that I have incorporated into my fusion cuisine, I think that you will find it quite simple to devise your own distinctive way with seasonings.

Spices

A dictionary definition of spice is "any of several vegetable substances used to season food." I find this a rather dry description of those tiny bits of something that are so fragrant, sensual, and visually appealing in texture and color and that add such intriguing complexity to our basic foods. I much prefer my definition of spices "magic elixirs that can be used as a remedy for all kitchen ailments." I often say that if I could be anything I would be saffron, or cardamom; saffron, as much for its intensely golden yellow color as for its pungency, and cardamom, for its gentle strength of flavor. I often find myself using these scents more frequently than any others.

Although most spices can now be found in supermarkets, I would suggest that you purchase yours in Indian, Pakistani, or other ethnic shops; specialty food stores; health food markets; or through mail order sources, where you are assured of a fairly quick turnover, which guarantees freshness.

Whenever possible, spices should be purchased whole, and stored, tightly covered and labeled, in a cool, dark, dry spot. Before they are used, most spices should be toasted, roasted, or fried (see page 17) before they are blended into a spice mixture or into a *masala* (an amalgam of warm spices, or spices and herbs, or spices, herbs, and aromatics). For grinding herbs and spices, traditionalists use a mortar and pestle or a grinding stone. However, I find that an inexpensive electric coffee grinder does the job beautifully. I keep one grinder for hot spices, one for sweet, and one that I use only for grinding cardamom, whose flavor is so pronounced.

Below you will find a list of spices that I consider essential. However, you don't have to buy out a spice store to start experimenting. Buy what you can comfortably cook with, and expand your stock as you expand your knowledge. Remember that most spices are considered to also be medicinal. I think it is important that you familiarize yourself with the properties of each so that, just like a pharmacist, you will be able to put together the perfect blend for your own kitchen remedy.

AJOWAN: The tiny, black seed of the carum plant, it resembles a poppy seed with a pungent aroma and sharp taste that suggest it should be used in moderation. I am particularly fond of its distinctive flavor, so I use it somewhat more frequently than is traditional in Indian cooking. If you are unable to find it, thyme or lovage or their oils can be substituted.

ANISE, ANISEED, AND STAR ANISE: Anise is a plant in the parsley family, having a sweetly delicate, licorice flavor. Aniseed is the tiny, light-brown, somewhat teardrop-shaped seed from this plant. It is used to add perfume to pilafs and stews as well as sweets. In France, it is the dominant flavor in the potent drink pastis. Star anise is a dried, dark-brown, star-shaped pod that contains tiny flavorful seeds in each section. It comes from a small evergreen tree. Although not related, both anise and star anise have quite similar, licorice-like flavors. Slightly bitterer than anise, star anise is used in the same manner as well as in drinks such as spiced teas.

ASAFETIDA: The dried resin from a rhizome grown only in Kashmir, Afghanistan, and Iran. It is sold in lump form as well as powdered, and to the uninitiated, it has an extremely noxious odor. Used in very small quantities (it works as a digestive), the cooked flavor has been likened to fusty onions or very mature garlic. The powder is always diluted with other powdered ingredients or flours, so I strongly recommend that you use only the lump form, which can be ground as needed. Once ground, asafetida powder will clump, so you should only grind as much as you need at one time. And be prepared for your entire house to fill with its distinctive aroma as you grind!

BLACK CUMIN SEEDS: Tiny, oblong, sweetly aromatic seeds harvested only in Kashmir and Iran that are used to add a delicate, almost herbal flavor to dishes. There is no substitute.

BLACK ONION SEEDS: Tiny, black, comma-shaped, shiny seeds of the nigella plant. They have no relationship, other than a resemblance, to onion seeds. Emitting a very robust earthy smell, black onion seeds are used in pickles, dals, and vegetable dishes and on nans and other breads. The seeds are also known in Indian markets as *kalonji*, and in Middle Eastern markets as *siyah danch*.

Cardamom Pods and Seeds: Cardamom pods are sold bleached, white, unbleached, a slightly mellow black, and pale green, which I find the most flavorful. The black seeds, which hold the fragrance, are inside the pods. Intensely sweet yet slightly spicy, green or black cardamom pods are generally used in savory dishes when a milder flavor is required (such as in pilafs), while the seeds are usually ground to give a more definitive flavor to desserts.

Cinnamon: The dried, inner bark of an evergreen tree, cinnamon can be purchased as sticks or powder. In Indian cooking, the whole stick is used to flavor meat or rice dishes as well as teas, but the powder is almost never used. Either form is sharply sweet with a slightly spicy bite.

Cloves: The dried, unopened buds of a tropical evergreen tree, deep, reddish-brown cloves add real fragrance and gusto to rice and grain recipes, tomato-based dishes, and desserts. May be purchased whole or ground.

Coriander Seeds: Resembling white peppercorns, coriander seeds are the dried fruit of a parsleylike plant. In its fresh form, coriander is also known as "cilantro" or "Chinese parsley." (The fresh and dried versions are not interchangeable.) Extremely aromatic, with a spicy, citruslike flavor, these seeds are used extensively in Indian cooking. They are also one of the primary components of the spice blends curry and *garam masala*. May be purchased whole or ground.

Cumin Seeds: Tiny, oblong, seeds that are the dried fruit of a parsleylike plant. They are either greenish-brown, white, or black (see "black cumin seeds," page 9). The first two are interchangeable in any recipe and have an intense, warm, and almost nutty aroma that instantly envokes Indian food. May be purchased whole or ground.

Fennel Seeds: Pale, greenish-yellow, oval seeds from the common fennel plant. Sweetly aromatic, these licoricelike seeds are used to flavor both sweet and savory dishes as well as liqueurs. Roasted fennel seeds are often chewed as a digestive after an Indian meal. May be purchased whole or ground.

FENUGREEK SEEDS: Rectangular, yellowish-brown, slightly bitter, yet warm and sweet, fenugreek seeds are actually legumes. However, because they are so aromatic and are frequently used to intensify the flavor of many Indian dishes, spice blends, and teas, they are usually referred to as a spice. Although I have never seen them in the United States, the leaves of the fenugreek plant may also be eaten, either cooked or raw. May be purchased whole or ground.

GINGER: A pale-brown, knobby rhizome, ginger is available fresh, dried (ground or in pieces), as preserved stem, and in crystallized form. Every form has a distinctly hot and tangy, yet refreshing flavor. Fresh ginger is often ground into a paste (a small food processor works well for this) or made into juice. To make ginger juice, puree 1 cup of chopped, peeled fresh ginger in a blender with 3 tablespoons of warm water. Press through a fine sieve, reserving the juice and discarding the solids. Ginger juice may be frozen.

MACE: The beautiful, deep reddish-brown, free-form outer coating of the nutmeg, available both ground and in blades. Its flavor is a bit more delicate than the slightly spicy pungency of nutmeg, while its color is more intense.

MUSTARD SEEDS: The tiny, round, hot and pungent seeds of the mustard plant are available in white, yellow, brown, or black. The larger white seeds are used to make commercial mustards in America; the yellow and brown ones are generally used in European mustards as well as for pickling; the black seeds are used primarily in Eastern cooking. I often use mustard seeds in place of the expected peppercorns. May be purchased whole or ground.

NUTMEG: The rich-brown seed of the fruit of a tropical evergreen, nutmeg has a warm, sweetly spicy flavor used to season both savory and sweet dishes. Although you can buy ground nutmeg, it is best to purchase whole seeds, which you can grate (on either a nutmeg or standard grater) as needed.

POMEGRANATE SEEDS: These sun-dried, kernel-like seeds of the wild Indian pomegranate are usually ground to give a lively, slightly tangy flavor to dishes. Fresh seeds of commercially grown pomegranates are not an acceptable substitute.

PEPPERCORNS: Very piquant, slightly hot berries that grow in grapelike clusters on the pepper plant. Dried peppercorns are available black or white. Black peppercorns are picked underripe and allowed to dry until dark and shriveled. They are the most strongly flavored of all peppercorns. White peppercorns are picked ripe, and the outer skins are removed before the peppercorns are dried, leaving light tan–colored berries. They are substantially less intense than the black ones and are often used to season light-colored sauces. Green peppercorns are underripe berries that have been cured in brine. Once rare, peppercorns are now one of the most common spices in American kitchens. May be purchased whole or ground.

SAFFRON: These intense yellow strands are the dried stigmas of a small purple crocus. Saffron is the world's most expensive spice, as it takes over 250,000 flowers to make one pound of saffron. It lends an extraordinary yellow color and distinct musky flavor to both savory and sweet dishes. Saffron is always an integral part of foods served at Indian religious festivals and weddings. May be purchased in strands or ground. For the sake of assured purity, I recommend threads because powdered saffron is often diluted with safflower or calendula or other ingredients.

TURMERIC: The dried rhizome of a gingerlike plant, intensely yellow ground turmeric is used to color many dishes and give that recognizable bright yellow color to curry spice blends. It has a rather bitter taste that, when cooked, becomes somewhat delicate, though musky.

Spice Blends

Curry Spice Blend

In India, there are as many curry spice blends as there are cooks! Although blends are commercially available (they're labeled "curry powder"), I don't recommend them. Since there is no standard mixture, you really can be a Merlin and create your own. Here is my recipe, which you should feel free to improve upon.

Makes about 1⅓ pounds

1 pound coriander seeds
¼ pound cumin seeds
1 tablespoon ground ginger
1 tablespoon sweet cumin seeds
1 tablespoon mustard seeds
1 tablespoon fenugreek
2 teaspoons ground turmeric
1 teaspoon whole cloves
One 2-inch cinnamon stick
2 cardamom seeds
8 black peppercorns
1 dried cayenne chile, seeded

1. Preheat the oven to 275°F.
2. Put all the ingredients on a large, low-sided baking sheet with sides and roast in the oven for 20 minutes, or until spices are lightly toasted and very aromatic.
3. Put the spice mixture in a spice grinder in batches, and process at high speed until spices are very finely ground. Pour into a nonreactive container with a lid. Cover tightly and store in a cool dark spot for no more than 3 months.

Garam Masala

This seasoning is an integral part of Indian and fusion cooking, yet there is no standard mixture for this aromatic mixture. Every cook in every region has a favorite recipe. Garam masala is also available commercially, but it imparts a much milder flavor than a homemade blend. Here is a favorite of mine.

Makes about ⅓ cup

3 tablespoons cardamom seeds
1 tablespoon black peppercorns
1 teaspoon whole cloves
1 teaspoon black cumin seeds
½ teaspoon coriander seeds
½ teaspoon freshly ground nutmeg
One 2-inch cinnamon stick
1 small dried cayenne chile, seeded

1. Preheat the oven to 275°F.
2. Put all the ingredients on a small, low-sided baking sheet and roast in the oven for 20 minutes, or until the spices are lightly toasted and very aromatic. Place in a spice grinder and process until very fine. Pour into a nonreactive container with a lid. Cover tightly and store in a cool, dark spot for no more than 3 months.

Oils and Fats

Although I keep a variety of fats and fruit and nut oils on hand at all times, the four that I use most frequently are ghee, olive oil, sesame oil, and peanut oil. When a recipe specifies a particular oil, I do suggest that you use it, as I have chosen it for a definite reason.

GHEE: Clarified butter, the traditional Indian fat used when a dish requires an additional rich, nutty taste or when the cook wishes to add just a hint of enrichment or smooth out the texture, just as one uses butter in classic French cooking. I often use ghee to sauté fish or delicately flavored meats and as an enrichment for sauces or as a seasoning for vegetables. To make ghee, slowly melt 1 pound of unsalted butter in a heavy-bottomed saucepan over very low heat. Bring it to a low boil and allow it to simmer for about 20 minutes, or until the white milk particles separate from the fat and begin to turn a golden brown. Remove from the heat and strain the fat through a triple layer of cheesecloth into a sterile container. Cover and store at room temperature. Ghee can be kept at least a week.

OLIVE OIL: My choice for smoothing out the texture of fruit sauces, making salad dressings, flavoring vegetable dishes, and occasionally sautéing or frying. I rarely use extra virgin olive oil, as its flavor is too fruity for the balance required in fusion cooking.

SESAME OIL: Used when a dish requires the sweet, nutty fragrance imparted by the rich, golden aromatic oil of sesame seeds. Indian sesame oil is milder than Chinese and much more aromatic than the pale oil readily available in supermarkets and health food stores. I use sesame oil to sauté vegetables, season sauces and condiments, and occasionally to heighten the flavor of a fish dish.

PEANUT OIL: My oil of choice for sautéing, frying, or blending when I want no flavor to be imparted to the dish. I prefer its clean, clear taste to that of other unflavored oils, such as corn, or to generic vegetable oil. It is also an excellent oil to use for the infusion of other flavors such as chiles or herbs.

INFUSED OILS: I keep an array of infused oils on hand. They are quite simple to make and are easy to store, tightly covered and refrigerated. All that is required is about 1 cup of peanut oil (or, occasionally, ghee), to which you add about 1 teaspoon of whatever dried spice, herb, chile, aromatic (onion, shallot, or garlic), or seasoning (for instance, ginger or tomatoes) you wish. Place the oil in a small saucepan over medium heat and cook until very hot but not smoking. Add the flavoring item. As soon as it begins to swell, brown, snap, crackle, or pop, remove the oil from the heat and allow it to cool. You can then either strain out the flavoring agent, or for stronger flavor, allow it to remain in the oil until ready to use. If the flavoring agent was fresh and you are going to leave it in the oil, the oil must be well sealed and refrigerated as soon as it has been prepared to prevent botulism from forming.

MUSTARD OIL: A common Indian frying fat. It is a rather bitter, mustard-flavored, bright yellow oil that adds an interesting dimension to vegetable dishes as well as to legumes.

Techniques

Each of the traditional Indian cooking techniques that I use has a clearly defined function in fusion cuisine. As you experiment and learn to incorporate them into your cooking, I think that you will understand their roles.

ROASTING OR TOASTING SPICES is a very simple way to encourage additional flavor from a spice. If a spice is used untoasted in one dish, toasting it will introduce an entirely different flavor into another dish on the table. Toasted or roasted whole spices will taste different from those that have been ground and then heated. Place the spices, one at a time, in a heavy-bottomed frying pan (cast iron is particularly good). You can either toast the spice on top of the stove over a medium flame or roast in a 300°F oven. The stovetop is preferable, as you can rotate and shake the pan, which keeps the spices from burning. The spice is done when it emits a lovely aroma and has turned about two shades darker. This is one time when practice does make perfect!

GRINDING OR CRUSHING SPICES should be done as required for a recipe. Use an inexpensive coffee grinder (see page 8), grinding one spice at a time. To remove any leftover spice, place a couple of teaspoons of sugar or salt in the grinder and wipe it clean with a slightly damp paper towel. If you do this after every use, there will be no aftertaste left in the grinder. Spices may be crushed with the flat blade of a knife.

BROWNING ONIONS is an age-old Indian method of thickening sauces without the addition of cream or butter. To brown onions properly, place oil in a nonstick sauté pan over medium-high heat. Add the specified amount of onions and sauté for about 5 minutes, or until onions begin to give off most of their liquid. Lower the heat and continue to cook, stirring occasionally, until the onions are a deep, reddish-brown color, but are not burned. A combination of aromatics, such as onions, garlic, and ginger, either chopped or in a paste form, or garlic by itself, can also be prepared in this manner.

MARINATING MEATS OR FISH can be done in two ways. I either coat the meat or fish in a dry rub comprised of a mixture of spices or spices and herbs, or in the traditional Indian manner, cut deep gashes in the meat or fish and then coat it in a mixture of yogurt and spices. The latter method allows for deep penetration of flavor and quick cooking. In addition, the yogurt works as a tenderizer, so I often use it on tough cuts of meat. Regardless of which method I use, I generally allow no less than 4 hours for the flavor to penetrate the meat or fish.

INFUSING ESSENCES into desserts is one of my favorite Indian techniques. I most often use rose or screw pine essence, in small quantities, to lift a dessert out of the ordinary by giving just a hint of the exotic.

FLAVORING WITH JAGGERY, or unrefined lump sugar, is more interesting to me than using regular granulated sugar. Jaggery, made from the juices of sugarcane or palm, is light brown in color and almost maplelike in flavor. It adds a very delicate and indefinable sweetness to desserts. If you can't find it, a combination of equal parts of dark brown and granulated white sugars and 1 tablespoon of maple sugar will make an excellent substitute.

PREPARING FRESH COCONUT MILK is an integral part of fusion cooking and is quite simple to do: Combine 1 cup of boiling water with 1 cup of tightly packed freshly grated coconut meat and let it rest for about 30 minutes. Then place the mixture in a blender and puree. Strain the puree through a double layer of cheesecloth, squeezing out as much of the liquid as possible, into a sterile container. You can also use frozen grated coconut to make fresh milk. Sweetened flaked coconut or canned coconut cream cannot be used as substitutes.

MAKING TAMARIND PULP is quite simple. Combine a 1-pound block of tamarind with 4 cups of cold water in a heavy saucepan over medium heat. Bring to a boil. Lower the heat and simmer for about 15 minutes, or until the tamarind is very soft. Pour into a blender and process until the mixture is of a soupy consistency, adding cold water, a bit at a time, if necessary. Strain the mixture through a medium sieve, pushing with a spatula, to separate the fibers and seeds from the pulp. Store the pulp in 1/2-cup amounts in the freezer. I find that small "zippered" plastic bags are perfect containers.

BLENDING SAUCES is the backbone of my cooking technique. All manner of fruit and vegetable sauces and vinaigrettes come flying out of my blenders. I almost never use a food processor, but I don't know what I would do without my commercial blender! When I make a new sauce or use a new combination of ingredients, I can look through the clear glass, checking the texture as I blend.

FIRING UP A RECIPE calls for a judicious use of fresh and dried chile peppers. Nowadays even the smallest supermarket seems to carry jalapeño and serrano chiles, which add wonderful, fresh, lusty spice to so many dishes. Fresh green and red chiles can be used interchangeably, but I do urge you to acquaint yourself with the degree of heat found in each type. Bell or sweet peppers are the mildest, and Scotch bonnets (or habañeros) are at the top of the heat scale. It is always a good idea to take extra care when cooking with chiles, as the oils can cause intense burning if you touch yourself with them. Wash your hands thoroughly after handling chiles. Dried chiles should be soaked in warm water for about 1 hour before use.

Wine Thoughts

At the risk of being called a snob, I have to admit that I truly love only French wines. Not that I haven't enjoyed a great many glasses of superb American wines or drunk my fair share of Italian, German, Australian, Chilean, Spanish, and other fruits of the vine. It is just that my heart (and palate) quite simply belongs to France! My taste for and love of French wine began long before my cooking career, so when I started to develop my own personal fusion style, it was only natural that wine pairing would be one of the joys of the experience. I believe that with my French-Indian fusion of techniques and flavors, the possibilities of wine complements are endless.

When I taste a wine by itself, I imagine all the flavors—spices, herbs, fruits, oils, emulsions—that will serve to showcase the wine. Although I love to study the physiology of wine, my greatest thrill is to be able to create a meal that allows the wine to blossom. In times past, when one cooked for a wine connoisseur, one assumed the food would nourish, but the wine would rule. From my viewpoint, this is no longer true. You must always keep in mind that both food and wine will taste quite different when served alone; it is through the cook's artistry that their marriage is one of love, not convenience.

In my own restaurant, we have had many memorable wine experiences. One particularly spectacular event was a venison celebration. I chose to prepare venison tenderloin in three distinct ways, each calling for its special complement. Serving a 1962 La Tâche, I coated the venison medallions with Provençal herbs and a rich, fruity olive oil, which took full advantage of the subtle complexities of this elegant Burgundy. For the 1989 Cos-d'Estournel, a Bordeaux, I created a plum puree made fragrant with a very, very small pinch of toasted cloves to sauce the venison. Since the wine is very fruity—filled with floral, cinnamon, and clove aromas—this was a perfect marriage. And a quite unforgettable melding on the palate! The 1992 Vieux Télégraphe, being a robust, hearty Châteauneuf-du-Pape, posed a bit of a challenge for building the necessary steps of complexity to meet it on equal terms. I prepared a ginger chutney with tamarind for acidity, toasted fenugreek for a taste of the exotic, and palm sugar to pull it all together. What a memorable evening it was!

As you cook your way through this book, I hope that you will use the wine suggestions to help lead you along your own path of memorable meals. When selecting wines, remember that it is often difficult to match wines precisely to soups and salads—soups, because of their consistency, and salads, because of their acidic dressings. With informed selections, you will find that each dish is enriched by the wine that you choose to serve with it. I know that your time at the table will be far more enjoyable if you lift a glass of great wine as a salute to your fine cooking.

RAJI

Crab Bisque with
Spices, and Ginger Juice

...tic Salmon with
...on Sauce

...h Curried

...ne

Lou...
La C...
$6...

Hors d'Oeuvres and Appetizers

Sevruga Caviar with Dal Blinis

Roulade of Tuna Tartare with Unfiltered Sesame
Oil and Brunois of Green Mango

Soft-Shell Crab with Cashew Crust and Carrot-
Ginger Chutney

Lemon-Cilantro Ceviche of Scallops

Crab Purses with Cumin-Scented Tomato Coulis

Crab Crustillant with Raspberry Sauce

Crisp Purses with Shrimp, Scallops, and Mint-
Ginger Sauce

Foie Gras with Fennel Seeds, Gratin of Ginger,
and Spring Asparagus

Foie Gras with French Lentils and Truffle Confit

Vegetable Purses with Cumin-Scented Tomatoes

Sevruga Caviar with Dal Blinis

Serves 6

1 cup *urad dal*, well washed and
    drained (see Note)

Coarse salt, to taste

3 tablespoons peanut oil
    (approximately)

6 ounces sevruga caviar or other fine
    quality caviar

18 small chive points

True fusion! Great caviar served on blinis made from dal, one of the legumes at the heart of Indian cooking. The subtle fragrance of the dal pancake complements the caviar particularly well. It amuses me to think of the everyday dal pancake, which I often had for breakfast as a child, as the base for the extravagant caviar. Spices are not added; they would overpower the caviar.

No Indian meal is complete without the ubiquitous dal. Whenever I can, I use one of the many dried pulses that add nutritious balance to much of the vegetarian cuisine of India. I love their flavors as much as I embrace their healthfulness.

1. Put the *urad dal* in a deep bowl with cold water to cover by about 3 inches. Using the palms of your hands, rub the dal to split them apart. Allow them to soak for at least 8 hours.

2. Drain well, reserving about half of the soaking water. Place the dal and half of the water into a food processor fitted with the metal blade. Process until very thick and smooth, adding additional soaking water as necessary. Add salt.

3. Pour 1 tablespoon of the oil in a nonstick griddle over medium heat, tilting the pan so the oil covers the entire bottom. When hot, pour spoonfuls of dal batter onto the griddle to make round blinis $2^{1}/_{2}$ inches in diameter. Do not crowd the pan. Cook for about 1 minute, or until the batter is set and the bottom is lightly browned. Turn the blinis and cook for an additional minute, or until they are cooked through.

Remove from the griddle, place on a warm plate, and loosely tent with foil to keep warm. Continue to grease the griddle and cook the blinis until you have 18.

4. Place 3 blinis, slightly overlapping, on each of 6 luncheon plates. Place a small spoonful of caviar in the center of each blini. Place a chive point into each mound of caviar and serve.

Note: Urad dal, or black gram beans, is available at Indian, Pakistani, or Middle Eastern markets, at some specialty food stores, or through one of the mail order sources listed on page 217.

Wine Suggestions: Taittinger Brut la Française
Iron Horse Brut
Both champagnes exhibit creaminess and richness that will enhance the flavors of the caviar and the dal blinis.

Roulade of Tuna Tartare with Unfiltered Sesame Oil and Brunois of Green Mango

Serves 6

2 hothouse (or English) cucumbers
   (see Note)
1 small firm green mango
3 pounds ice-cold sushi-grade
   yellowfin tuna (see Note)
1 fresh cayenne chile, stemmed,
   seeded, and finely minced
1 tablespoon chopped cilantro
1 tablespoon chopped fresh curry
   leaves
1 tablespoon Vietnamese chili sauce
1 tablespoon crushed toasted cumin
   seeds
1/4 cup unfiltered sesame seed oil
1 teaspoon wasabi caviar
1 teaspoon orange-flavored caviar
18 sprigs cilantro, well-washed,
   trimmed, and dried

The first time I made this dish, I made it for lunch for myself. It was a terribly hot and humid Memphis day that called for something light yet flavorful. I was so pleased with my invention that it ended up in the amuse-bouche that evening and then became a staple on the menu.

As an appetizer, these roulades are spectacular. As an hors d'oeuvre, you'll need to make them a bit smaller by cutting the cucumber slices in half lengthwise and then crosswise, so that you create just a tidbit. The wasabi- and orange-flavored caviar garnishes, available at Japanese markets, are the same ones that are used in sushi bars. They are inexpensive fish roe that have been colored and flavored, which adds drama and crunch to the finished dish.

1. Wash the cucumbers and pat dry. Using a meat slicer, slice the cucumbers lengthwise into 12 very thin slices of equal length, reserving the remaining cucumber for another use. Set aside.
2. Peel the mango and cut it into 1/4-inch dice. Set aside.
3. Clean the tuna, making sure to remove all skin and connective tissue. Using a sharp knife, cut the tuna into 1/4-inch dice. Place in a nonreactive mixing bowl. Add the chile, cilantro, curry leaves, chili sauce, cumin, and the reserved diced mango. Drizzle the oil over the top and toss lightly to combine.
4. Lay the cucumber slices on a clean counter. Place an equal portion of the tuna mixture at the top of each slice. One at a

time, roll up the cucumber slices to make a neat, tight roulade. If the end of the cucumber does not lay flat, using a sharp knife, trim the edge on the diagonal and press it into the roll.

5. Place 2 roulades, upright, on each of 6 luncheon plates. Place a dab of wasabi caviar on one side of the top of each roulade, and a portion of orange-flavored caviar on the other side, mounding slightly. Nestle 3 sprigs of cilantro between the roulades, and serve immediately.

Note: I suggest that you purchase 2 cucumbers to allow for a reserve in case you have breakage (as I often do) as you cut the very thin slices.

Three pounds of expensive sushi-grade tuna might seem like a lot for this recipe, but I find that I lose a great deal when I clean the fish of all connective tissue. I am pretty insistent on this, as I think that there is nothing more unpleasant than finding chewy pieces of raw fish. The colder the tuna is, the easier it will be to cut off the connective tissue and dice the remaining fish. To get the fish to a nicely chilled slicing consistency, put it into the freezer for about 15 minutes before cutting.

Wine Suggestions: Sanford Pinot Noir
Louis Jadot Gevrey-Chambertin
The sweet fruit of the Pinot Noir grape marries well with the unctuous tuna.

Soft-Shell Crab with Cashew Crust and Carrot-Ginger Chutney

Serves 6

1/2 cup canola oil

1/4 teaspoon mustard seeds

1/2 cup *chana dal* (see Note)

3 carrots, peeled and coarsely chopped

1 tablespoon minced fresh ginger

1/2 teaspoon ground coriander seeds

1 cup buttermilk

1 cup water (approximately)

Coarse salt, to taste

1 cup finely ground cashew nuts

1 teaspoon ground cayenne

1/4 teaspoon ground cumin

1/4 cup ghee (see page 15)

6 soft-shell crabs, well cleaned

1 1/2 cups fresh fennel fronds (optional)

Carrot-ginger chutney transports me back to my childhood. I remembered the taste when thinking of accompaniments for soft-shell crab, and I just knew that the flavors would be a great match. I'm always amazed when something that I have "tasted" in my mind translates so well on the plate. For the few weeks that soft-shell crab are at their very best, this is a constant on my menu, with the cashew crust adding some complexity to the sweet crab taste.

1. To make the chutney, heat 1/4 cup of the oil in a large sauté pan over medium heat. Add the mustard seeds and sauté for about 2 minutes, or until the seeds begin to brown and pop and are very aromatic. Add the *chana dal* and sauté for about 3 minutes, or until the dal begins to brown. Stir in the carrots and continue to cook, stirring frequently, for about 6 minutes, or until the carrots just begin to soften. Remove from the heat and stir in the ginger and 1/4 teaspoon of the coriander.

2. Scrape the carrot mixture into a blender. Add the buttermilk and begin to process, adding water as necessary to make a very smooth puree. Taste and adjust seasoning with salt. Set aside.

3. Combine the ground cashews, cayenne, cumin, and remaining coriander in a small bowl. Stir in the ghee. When well combined, generously coat each crab with the cashew mixture.

4. Heat the remaining oil in a large skillet over medium-high heat. Add the crab, without crowding the pan, and sauté,

turning frequently, for about 4 minutes, or until the crab is crisp and lightly browned. Do this in batches if necessary.

5. Pour about ¼ cup of the carrot-ginger chutney into the center of each of 6 warm luncheon plates. If desired, make a bed of fennel fronds in the center of the plate. Place a crab in the center and serve, with the remaining chutney passed on the side.

Note: Chana dal *(yellow split peas) is available at Indian or Pakistani markets, in some specialty food stores, or through one of the sources listed on page 209.*

Wine Suggestions: Trimbach Pinot Gris
King Estate Pinot Gris
The flavor of the Pinot Gris grape complements the various flavors of this exotic dish.

Lemon-Cilantro Ceviche of Scallops

Serves 6

1/4 teaspoon mustard seeds

1/4 teaspoon cumin seeds

1 teaspoon peanut oil

3 cups water

Coarse salt, to taste

3 tablespoons fresh lemon juice

6 large fresh sea scallops

1/3 cup chopped fresh cilantro

1 small fresh cayenne chile, stemmed, seeded, and minced

1/2 cup finely sliced red radishes

The humid Memphis weather often takes its toll when I am in the kitchen, so I try to think of dishes that will be tasty, yet easy to prepare. This is one such dish—as easy to make as it is to serve! Just be sure that you have purchased extremely fresh scallops, so that their delicately sweet flavor is nicely showcased by the spices, cilantro, and chile.

1. Place the mustard and cumin seeds in a medium saucepan over medium heat. Cook, stirring constantly, for about 2 minutes, or until the seeds begin to pop. Stir in the oil. Add the water and salt and bring to a boil. Remove the pan from the heat and allow the mixture to cool to room temperature. Stir in the lemon juice and set aside.

2. When ready to serve, thinly slice 1 scallop into each of 6 shallow soup bowls. Pour 1/2 cup of the cooled lemon-spice water over the scallop in each cup. Gently stir in some of the cilantro and chile, sprinkle radish slices over the top, and serve.

Wine Suggestions: Cloudy Bay Sauvignon Blanc
Château Sancerre
The Sauvignon sings a high note against this simple heat-filled seafood dish.

Crab Purses with Cumin-Scented Tomato Coulis

Serves 6

3 medium very ripe tomatoes

5 tablespoons canola oil

1/4 teaspoon toasted ground cumin

Coarse salt, to taste

2 cups finely julienned cabbage

1/2 teaspoon ground red chile
  powder

1/4 teaspoon ground turmeric

14 ounces fresh crabmeat, picked
  over to remove cartilage

9 sheets phyllo dough

1/2 cup ghee (see page 15)

18 fresh chives (see Note)

6 pansies or other edible flowers, well
  washed and dried

Crab is a favorite seafood of so many of my guests that I am always trying to come up with a new way to bring it to my menu. Originally I made these purses as tiny one-bite hors d'oeuvres for a private party. The crunch of the phyllo contrasts with the meltingly sweet crab filling, to make each purse a sensory explosion on the tongue. The tomato coulis adds a nice acidic touch to complete the gustatory picture.

1. Core and finely dice the tomatoes, reserving the juice.

2. Heat 3 tablespoons of the oil in a medium sauté pan over medium heat. Add the tomatoes with the reserved juice and sauté for about 2 minutes, or just until they begin to soften. Transfer to a blender and add the cumin and salt. Process until very smooth. Set aside.

3. Preheat the oven to 450°F.

4. Heat the remaining oil in a nonstick sauté pan over medium-high heat. Add the cabbage, chile powder, and turmeric. Season with salt. Sauté for 3 minutes, or until the cabbage begins to wilt. Stir in the crabmeat and continue to sauté for about 2 minutes, or until the crabmeat is heated through. Remove from the heat and set aside.

5. Working quickly, cut 3 sheets of phyllo dough in half. Keep three halves and the remaining whole sheets tightly covered with plastic wrap. Using a pastry brush, lightly coat the surface of a half-sheet with ghee, top it with another half-sheet, and lightly coat the surface with ghee. Place the final half-sheet on

top and coat it with ghee. Place 3 tablespoons of the crab mixture in the center of the stacked phyllo sheets. Fold over the two long sides to cover the crab. Fold over the shorter sides to make a neat package. Turn it over so the folded edges are on the bottom. Tie one chive around two sides of the package and knot it at the center of the top. Tie another chive around the opposite sides and knot it at the center. You should now have a neat bundle that resembles a wrapped package. Using the pastry brush, carefully coat the entire package with ghee. Place the finished package on a baking sheet lined with parchment paper, and continue making packages as described above, until you have 6 bundles.

6. Bake the packages for 10 minutes, or until golden brown.

7. Spoon 2 tablespoons of the tomato coulis into the center of each of 6 luncheon plates. Place a crab purse in the center with a pansy tucked into the side. Serve warm.

Note: The purses and the coulis can be made early in the day. The purses should be refrigerated until ready to bake, while the coulis can be left at room temperature until ready to serve.

I have listed more chives than needed to allow for the inevitable breakage. It is often easier to tie them if they have first been dipped in extremely hot water and then dipped in ice water. Pat them dry before attempting to tie.

Wine Suggestions: Pascal Jolivet Sancerre
Campanile Pinot Grigio
Both wines exhibit nice acidity to handle the spice-and-crab combination.

Crab Crustillant with Raspberry Sauce

Serves 6

6 cups ultrafine Indian vermicelli (see Note)

1 1/4 cups ghee (see page 15)

1/4 teaspoon mustard seeds

3/4 cup fresh raspberries

3/4 pound lump crabmeat, picked over to remove cartilage

3/4 pound St. André cheese (or other mild soft cheese, see Note)

1 teaspoon finely chopped fennel fronds

1/4 cup Turmeric Oil (see page 13)

2 tablespoons sevruga caviar (optional)

This recipe—one of my most requested—looks rather like a fat porcupine ball! It was inspired by a few days I spent in Jean-Louis Palladin's kitchen, which left me bursting with new ideas. I first made it for an event at the James Beard House, in New York City, and just before the event, I created a surprise special lunch for Jean-Louis and some other chefs in the kitchen of Restaurant Daniel to give it a trial run. I couldn't fool Jean-Louis—one taste and he shouted, "Raji's in the kitchen working her fusion magic!"

1. Preheat the oven to 500°F.

2. Line 2 low-sided baking pans with parchment paper.

3. Spread 2 cups of the vermicelli on 1 of the prepared baking sheets. Place in the preheated oven and bake for 3 minutes, or until just golden. Remove from the oven and set aside.

4. Heat 1/4 cup of the ghee in a medium sauté pan over medium heat. Add the mustard seeds and sauté for 2 minutes. Gently stir in the raspberries, taking care that you don't break them apart. Cook for about 2 minutes, or until the raspberries are quite soft, but not mushy. Remove from the heat and cover to keep warm.

5. Spread the remaining vermicelli on the second baking pan. Set aside.

6. In a medium-size mixing bowl, using a wooden spoon, thoroughly combine the crabmeat, cheese, and fennel fronds. Shape the mixture into 6 balls of equal size.

7. Roll the crab balls in the reserved untoasted vermicelli to cover them completely. Place the vermicelli-covered crab balls

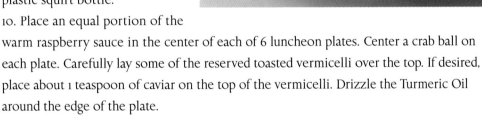

on the baking pan lined with uncooked vermicelli. Drizzle the balls generously with the remaining ghee, making certain that they are completely covered.

8. Place the balls in the preheated oven and bake for 2 minutes, or until the vermicelli is golden and the cheese has softened slightly. (You don't want the cheese to be runny.)

9. Pour the Turmeric Oil in a plastic squirt bottle.

10. Place an equal portion of the warm raspberry sauce in the center of each of 6 luncheon plates. Center a crab ball on each plate. Carefully lay some of the reserved toasted vermicelli over the top. If desired, place about 1 teaspoon of caviar on the top of the vermicelli. Drizzle the Turmeric Oil around the edge of the plate.

Note: If you can't find the Indian vermicelli that makes this dish so fascinating to look at (as well as eat!), try shredded phyllo dough for almost the same effect.

Although the St. André works particularly well with the crab, any soft mild cheese can be substituted—even plain old cream cheese will do the job nicely.

Wine Suggestions: Michel Lynch Bordeaux Blanc
Dry Creek Fumé Blanc
Sauvignon Blanc is the perfect accompaniment to this very rich, slightly sweet dish.

Crisp Purses with Shrimp, Scallops, and Mint-Ginger Sauce

Serves 6

2 cups urad dal, well washed and
  drained (see Note)

1 cup rice flour

Coarse salt, to taste

1/2 cup peeled, cored, seeded, and
  diced very ripe plum tomatoes

1 cup fresh mint leaves

1 tablespoon minced fresh ginger

1/4 cup dry white wine

1/4 cup olive oil

2 tablespoons ghee (approximately,
  see page 15)

1/4 cup peanut oil

1/4 cup finely diced onion

12 jumbo shrimp, peeled and
  deveined

12 large fresh sea scallops

Urad dal and rice flour combine to make a traditional breakfast dish in South India. I have taken this standard and, I hope, improved upon it. The crêpes for the purses are paper thin and crispy, yet pliable enough to quickly mold while hot. This takes a little patience, but don't give up—it is a very sensual dish! My fiancé, Lou, says it sealed our fate!

Urad dal has the most wonderful fragrance, which seems to harmonize marvelously with the delicacy of fish and shellfish. However, I also make smaller crêpes and serve them simply, with some warm ghee and chopped chives.

1. Put the *urad dal* in a deep bowl with water to cover by about 3 inches. Allow to soak for at least 8 hours or overnight. Place the *urad dal* and soaking water in a blender and process to a very fine puree. Add the rice flour and enough water (usually no more than 2 cups) to make a crêpelike batter the consistency of heavy cream. Blend in salt.

2. Combine 1/4 cup of the tomatoes with the mint, ginger, wine, and olive oil in a blender. Process, using quick on-and-off turns, to a consistency of salsa. Taste and adjust seasoning with salt. Set aside.

3. With a pastry brush, lightly coat a nonstick griddle with ghee. Place over medium-high heat. When hot, pour enough dal batter onto the griddle to make a paper-thin, 6-inch crêpe. Cook for about 1 minute, or until the batter has set and the bottom is lightly browned. Turn the crêpe and cook for an

additional minute, or until the crêpe has just set. Working very quickly and carefully, since the crêpe crisps almost immediately, remove it from the griddle and fold up the sides to make a small basket shape. You should have a very crisp, *tuile*like crêpe that holds its shape once formed. Continue to make crêpes as described above until you have made a total of 6 baskets.

4. Heat the peanut oil in a large sauté pan over medium-high heat. Add the onions and the remaining tomatoes and sauté for 3 minutes, or until the vegetables have softened. Add the shrimp and scallops and continue to sauté for about 3 minutes, or just until the shellfish are cooked through (the scallops can remain a bit raw in the center, if you like).

5. Place 1 basket on each of 6 luncheon plates. Spoon an equal portion of the shellfish mixture into the center of each basket. Drizzle mint-ginger sauce around the edge of the plate and over the top of the shellfish in the basket. Serve immediately.

Note: Urad dal *(black gram beans) is available at Indian, Pakistani, or Middle Eastern markets, at some specialty food stores, or through one of the sources listed on page 209.*

Wine Suggestions: La Foret Blanc
Michel Picard Chablis
French Chardonnay is a nice complement to the complexity of flavors in this well-seasoned seafood combination.

Foie Gras with Fennel Seeds, Gratin of Ginger, and Spring Asparagus

Serves 6

2 tablespoons fennel seeds

¹/₄ cup dry white wine

One 1-pound Grade A foie gras (see Note)

1 cup finely julienned asparagus

1 cup *chana dal* flour (see Note)

¹/₂ cup palm sugar

2 tablespoons finely chopped fresh ginger

¹/₄ cup plus 2 teaspoons ghee (see page 15)

Coarse salt and freshly ground pepper, to taste

I seem to have made my mark with foie gras, and this is one of my favorite flavor combinations. The intensity of the ginger and palm sugar within the *chana dal* crust is a perfect contrast to the rich, mellow foie gras. The wine-scented fennel seeds add the final burst of flavor on the palate. The inspiration for the gratin came from a very crisp South Indian dessert made from *chana dal* flour, sugar, and ghee.

1. Combine the fennel seeds with the wine in a small nonreactive container. Cover and set aside to marinate for about 30 minutes.

2. Using a very sharp knife, separate the foie gras lobes by cutting the connecting tendon. For this recipe, you will only need the larger lobe, so reserve the remaining lobe for another use, such as a pâté or a mousse.

3. Carefully remove all the veins, taking care not to smash the liver. Place the cleaned lobe on a dry, cool surface and, using a very sharp knife dipped in boiling water, cut at a slight angle, to make a ⁵/₈ to ³/₄-inch-thick slice of foie gras weighing about 3 ounces. Continue cutting in the same manner, dipping the knife into the boiling water each time you use it, until you have 6 slices of equal size. Lay each slice flat and, using a clean cloth, pat it dry. Place the foie gras slices on a plate and cover with plastic film. Refrigerate until ready to cook.

4. Put the asparagus in a small saucepan filled with boiling water to cover, and blanch for about 30 seconds, or just until

the color is set. Drain immediately and refresh under cold running water. Pat dry and set aside.

5. Preheat the oven to 450°F.

6. Combine the *chana dal* flour, sugar, and ginger with ¹/₄ cup of ghee in a medium, ovenproof, nonstick sauté pan and stir until well blended. Bake, stirring frequently, for about 5 minutes, or until a nicely toasted crumble has formed. Remove from the oven, and set aside to come to room temperature.

7. Place a medium nonstick sauté pan over high heat. Do not oil the pan. Remove the foie gras from the refrigerator and unwrap it. Season both sides with salt and pepper. When the pan is very hot, add the foie gras. Using your fingertips, gently push the slices into the pan so that the foie gras slices immediately begin to render their fat. Cook for about 2 minutes, or until the bottoms begin to caramelize and quite a bit of the fat has been rendered out. Turn and sear the other sides for about 2 minutes, or until the outsides are crisp. Using a slotted spoon, lift the foie gras from the pan and place on a warm plate.

8. Heat the remaining 2 teaspoons of ghee in a medium nonstick sauté pan. Add the reserved asparagus and sauté for about 1 minute, or just until it is warm. Remove from the heat and season with salt and pepper.

9. Uncover and drain the fennel seeds. Pat dry.

10. Place a slice of foie gras on each of 6 luncheon plates. Sprinkle some of the fennel seeds over the foie gras. Lightly sprinkle the ginger gratin over each slice of foie gras and around the edge of the plate. Arrange equal portions of the asparagus on each plate and serve.

Note: Foie gras is available at specialty food stores or by mail order from D'Artagnan, listed under Sources on page 209.

Chana dal flour is available at Indian, Pakistani, or Middle Eastern markets, at some specialty food stores, or through one of the sources listed on page 209.

Wine Suggestions: Château Greysac
Laurel Glen Terra Rosa
A Cabernet-base wine mixes well with this dish, which has an explosion of flavor on the tongue.

Foie Gras with French Lentils and Truffle Confit

Serves 6

2 cups French lentils (lentilles du Puy)

$1/4$ cup sliced truffles (about 1 ounce; see Note)

6 tablespoons plus 2 teaspoons olive oil

$1/4$ cup minced shallots

1 cup clam juice

$1/4$ teaspoon ground coriander

Coarse salt and freshly ground black pepper, to taste

One 1-pound Grade A foie gras (see Note)

Guests at Restaurant Raji always expect foie gras to be on the menu. This popular dish is heady with the fragrances of the French table. The pungent truffles add just the right note of extravagant earthiness to this extremely rich and expensive dish. Save it for those very special occasions when cost is not a concern.

1. Put the lentils in a medium saucepan with cold water to cover by at least 1 inch. Add 6 truffle slices and allow to soak for 8 hours or overnight.

2. Remove the truffle slices from the lentils. Pat dry and combine them with the remaining truffle slices.

3. Place the lentils over medium heat and bring to a boil. Lower the heat and simmer for about 20 minutes, or until the lentils are very soft. Remove from the heat and set aside.

4. Set aside 18 truffle slices. Combine the remaining slices with 6 tablespoons of the olive oil in a blender. Process until smooth. Set aside.

5. Heat the remaining olive oil in a medium sauté pan over medium heat. Add the shallots and sauté for about 5 minutes, or until the shallots are translucent but not brown. Scrape the shallots into the lentils. Stir in the clam juice, coriander, and the truffle puree. Place the pan over medium heat and bring to a boil. Lower the heat and simmer for about 15 minutes, or until the mixture is quite thick and smooth, adding water, 1 or 2 tablespoons at a time, as needed. Taste and adjust the seasoning

with salt and pepper. Remove from the heat. Cover and keep warm.

6. Using a very sharp knife, separate the foie gras lobes by cutting the connecting tendon. For this recipe, you will only need the larger lobe, so reserve the remaining lobe for another use, such as a pâté or a mousse.

7. Carefully remove all of the veins, taking care not to smash the liver. Place the cleaned lobe on a dry, cool surface and, using a very sharp knife dipped in boiling water, cut at a slight angle, to make a $5/8$ to $3/4$-inch-thick slice of foie gras weighing about 3 ounces. Continue cutting in the same manner, dipping the knife into the boiling water each time you use it, until you have 6 slices of equal size. Lay each slice flat and, using a clean cloth, pat it dry.

8. Place a medium nonstick sauté pan over high heat. Do not oil the pan. Season both sides of the foie gras with salt and pepper. When the pan is very hot, add the foie gras. Using your fingertips, gently push the slices into the pan, so that the foie gras slices immediately begin to render their fat. Cook for about 2 minutes, or until the bottoms begin to caramelize and quite a bit of the fat has been rendered out. Turn and sear the other sides for about 2 minutes, or until the outsides are crisp. Using a slotted spoon, lift the foie gras from the pan and place on a warm plate.

9. Pour equal portions of the lentil puree into each of 6 shallow soup bowls. Lay a piece of foie gras into the center of each bowl. Break 3 truffle slices over each portion and serve immediately.

Note: Foie gras is available at specialty food stores or by mail order from D'Artagnan, listed under Sources, on page 209. Truffles and lentilles du Puy are available from some specialty food stores or by mail order from one of the merchants listed on page 209.

Wine Suggestions: Bonny Doon Muscat Vin de Glacière
Lindemans Griffin Semillon
Both of these full-bodied wines can handle this ultrarich dish equally well.

Vegetable Purses with Cumin-Scented Tomatoes

Serves 6

1 tablespoons plus 2 teaspoons peanut oil

¼ teaspoon minced garlic

¼ teaspoon minced serrano chile

½ cup finely chopped cabbage

¼ cup finely chopped carrot

¼ cup finely chopped zucchini

Coarse salt and freshly ground black pepper, to taste

1 cup ¼-inch dice of peeled, cored, and seeded very ripe yellow tomatoes

¼ teaspoon freshly crushed toasted cumin seeds

6 sheets phyllo dough

¼ cup ghee (see page 15)

¼ pound mixed baby salad greens, well washed and dried

6 nasturtium or chive flowers, well washed and dried

This might be considered a fusion version of the traditional Indian samosa (one of my favorite snacks). The crisp vegetable filling has just a hint of heat and spice, creating an enticing introduction to an aromatic meal. Although the chives make a charming packet, they are not absolutely necessary to complete the dish.

1. Line a low-sided baking sheet with sides with parchment paper. Set aside.

2. Heat 1 tablespoon of the peanut oil in a large sauté pan over medium heat. Add the garlic and chile and sauté for 1 minute. Stir in the cabbage, carrot, and zucchini and sauté for about 3 minutes or just until the vegetables have wilted slightly. Season with salt and pepper. Remove from the heat and set aside.

3. Heat the remaining 2 teaspoons of peanut oil in a medium sauté pan over medium heat. Add the tomatoes, cumin, and salt and sauté for about 3 minutes, or until tomatoes are quite soft. Remove from the heat and puree in a blender. Set aside.

4. Preheat the oven to 450°F.

5. Cover the phyllo sheets with a slightly dampened kitchen towel. Using a pastry brush, lightly coat a sheet with ghee. Fold the ghee-covered sheet in half and lightly coat the top of the folded sheet with more ghee. Place about 3 tablespoons of the vegetable mixture in the center of the sheet. Fold over the 2 long sides to cover the vegetable mixture. Fold over the shorter sides to make a neat roll. Place the folded edges on the bottom.

You should now have a neat bundle that resembles a Chinese egg roll. Using the pastry brush, carefully coat the entire package with ghee. Place the finished package on the prepared baking sheet and continue making packages as above until you have 6 wrapped packages.

6. Bake the packages for 10 minutes, or until golden brown.

7. Spoon about 3 tablespoons of the cumin-scented tomato sauce into the center of each of 6 luncheon plates. Cut the vegetable rolls in half, on the diagonal. Place the 2 halves, standing upright, in the center of the plate, with a handful of baby greens and an edible flower nestled into them. Serve warm.

Note: The purses can be made early in the day and stored, covered and refrigerated. Bake just before serving.

For smaller cocktail-size tidbits, cut the phyllo sheets in half.

I have listed more chives than needed to allow for the inevitable breakage.

Wine Suggestions: Duckhorn Sauvignon Blanc
Buena Vista Sauvignon Blanc
The crisp Sauvignon Blanc makes a perfect partner, highlighting the spiced vegetable filling of these purses.

Soups

Crab Soup with Sweet Spices and Ginger Juice

Shrimp Bisque

Consommé of Green Apricots with Belle
   Shrimp

Broccoli and Green Pea Soup with Indian Curry
   Leaves and Mustard Seeds

Coconut Milk Soup with Lobster and Toasted
   Poppy Seeds

Carrot-Saffron Soup

Chilled Cucumber Soup with Dill and Mustard
   Seeds

Velouté of Curried Butternut Squash Soup

Tamarind Consommé

*No wine pairings are offered in this chapter because I find it very hard to match wines to soups
effectively. I suggest that you drink your favorite white wine with any of my soup or consommé
selections, or you might also want to offer whatever wine you are serving with your entree.*

Crab Soup
with Sweet Spices and Ginger Juice

Serves 6

3/4 pound jumbo lump crabmeat,
  picked over to remove cartilage
1 fresh cayenne chile
3 tablespoons canola oil
1 large clove garlic, blanched and
  minced
1 tablespoon finely chopped onion
2 teaspoons Garam Masala
  (see page 14)
2 tablespoons fresh ginger juice
  (see page 12)
1 teaspoon saffron powder
4 cups heavy cream
Coarse salt, to taste

This fusion soup evolved from a soup our cook, Mrs. Ayyer, made when I was a child. It combines the richness of a classic French bisque with the zest and energy of Indian spices to create a marvelous sensation on the tongue. I use ginger juice because minced fresh ginger would overwhelm the mellow crab. It is a luxurious soup that should not be served every day!

1. Set aside $1/4$ cup of the crabmeat for a garnish.
2. Wash the chile and remove the stem. Cut the chile in half crosswise and mince the top half only. Reserve the bottom for another use.
3. Heat the oil in a large heavy-bottomed saucepan over medium heat. Add the garlic, onion, and minced chile. Sauté for about 3 minutes, or just until vegetables begin to brown slightly. Stir in the garam masala. When well combined, add the ginger juice. Stir well again. Add the larger portion of the crabmeat and bring to a simmer again. Simmer for 5 minutes, stirring gently from time to time. Stir in the saffron and simmer for an additional minute. Add the cream and bring to a simmer again. Lower the heat and allow the soup to just barely simmer for about 15 minutes, or until it is slightly reduced. Taste and adjust seasoning with salt, if necessary.
4. Pour an equal portion into each of 6 shallow soup bowls. Garnish the center of each serving with some of the reserved crabmeat and serve immediately.

Shrimp Bisque

Serves 6

2 ½ cups heavy cream

1 cup half-and-half

1 small onion, peeled and chopped

½ teaspoon minced jalapeño chile

2 tablespoons Garam Masala (see page 14)

Large pinch saffron threads

Pinch ground turmeric

Coarse salt, to taste

1 pound tiny shrimp, cooked, peeled, and deveined (See Note)

6 small sprigs fresh cilantro

People in the South are crazy about shrimp, so I always try to have a shrimp dish on my menu. To me, tiny shrimp are so much sweeter and tastier than the large ones. Here the spices add interest without overpowering the delicate shrimp. I call this soup a "bisque," but it is actually just a bit of mysteriously flavored cream moistening the little shrimp. These delicate tastes seduce the diner into the meal.

1. Combine the cream, half-and-half, onion, chile, garam masala, saffron, and turmeric in a deep, nonreactive saucepan over medium-low heat. Bring to a boil; then immediately remove from the heat. Allow to steep for 30 minutes. Taste and adjust the seasoning with salt. Set aside.

2. When ready to serve, divide the shrimp equally among 6 small, shallow soup bowls. Return the cream mixture to medium-high heat and cook for about 1 minute, or until bubbles form around the sides of the pan. Remove from the heat and strain through a fine sieve into a clean container. Pour an equal portion of the cream mixture over the shrimp in each bowl. Place a sprig of cilantro in the center and serve.

Note: If you can't find tiny shrimp, use whatever size is available and cut the shrimp into bite-size pieces.

Consommé of Green Apricots with Belle Shrimp

Serves 6

1 tablespoon peanut oil

2 tablespoons minced shallots

1/2 teaspoon toasted ground coriander

1/2 teaspoon toasted freshly ground black pepper

20 very firm, unripe apricots, washed, halved, and pitted

4 cups cold water

Coarse salt, to taste

2 cups Belle or other medium shrimp, cooked, peeled, and deveined

6 sprigs fresh thyme, leaves only

Here tart, unripe apricots make a very refreshing consommé, and spices add an extra zing. I devised this soup when I received a shipment of what were supposed to be "tree-ripened apricots." I find that most apricots are sold unripe and never seem to attain the sweet, luscious goodness that I crave. This refreshingly tropical soup is a constant on my summer menu. The sweet baby shrimp and aromatic thyme round out the soup perfectly, to make a colorful yet delicate dish.

1. Heat the oil in medium saucepan over medium heat. Add the shallots and sauté for about 3 minutes, or just until they are soft. Stir in the coriander and pepper and sauté for 1 minute. Add the apricots and sauté for about 5 minutes, or just until the apricots are soft, taking care not to brown the fruit.

2. Scrape the apricot mixture into a blender and puree. With the motor running, add the water and salt and process until the mixture is very smooth. Pour into a clean saucepan and return to low heat. Bring to a simmer; then remove from the heat.

3. Put the shrimp in warm water to cover about 1 minute or less to just heat through. Drain well and pat dry.

4. Pour an equal portion of the apricot consommé into each of 6 shallow soup bowls. Gently stir some of the shrimp into each bowl. Sprinkle some thyme leaves over the top and serve.

Broccoli and Green Pea Soup with Indian Curry Leaves and Mustard Seeds

Serves 6

1 bunch broccoli

2 cups fresh peas, or frozen tiny peas

2 tablespoons peanut oil

1 teaspoon Curry Spice Blend (page 14) or curry powder

1/4 teaspoon mustard seeds

1/4 teaspoon cumin seeds

4 cups water

Coarse salt, to taste

20 fresh curry leaves, julienned

When I was a recent immigrant, I would get so homesick for Indian food but couldn't always find the ingredients to make it. Our cook, Mrs. Ayyer, had packed some mustard and cumin seeds and chiles for me, saying, "As long as you have tempered spices, you can give anything a Brahmin touch."

1. Wash the broccoli and cut the top into very small florets, reserving the stems for another use (such as a broccoli puree or cream soup). Place the florets in a pot filled with boiling salted water to cover and blanch for 30 seconds. Drain and refresh under cold running water. Pat dry and set aside.

2. Put the peas in a blender or food processor fitted with the metal blade and puree. Scrape the puree into a fine strainer and push it through with a spatula to strain out any tough skin. Set puree aside.

3. Heat the oil in a large saucepan over medium-high heat. Add the curry powder and mustard and cumin seeds. Sauté for about 3 minutes, or until the seeds begin to take on color and are very aromatic. Add the reserved broccoli florets and pea puree and stir to combine. Stirring constantly, add the water and salt. When well combined, bring to a boil. Immediately remove from the heat and stir in the curry leaves.

4. Pour an equal portion of the soup into each of 6 shallow soup bowls and serve hot.

Coconut Milk Soup
with Lobster and Toasted Poppy Seeds

Serves 6

¹/₄ cup canola oil

2 tablespoons finely chopped shallots

¹/₄ cup chopped cilantro

1 tablespoon minced fresh ginger

¹/₂ teaspoon toasted poppy seeds

¹/₄ teaspoon toasted ground cloves

¹/₄ teaspoon toasted ground
cinnamon

¹/₄ teaspoon ground turmeric

Two 2-inch pieces tender lemongrass
stalk, tied together with a chive

1 pound fresh lobster meat, cut into
chunks

One 14-ounce can coconut milk

2 cups heavy cream

Coarse salt, to taste

At the risk of contradicting myself about soups not pairing well with wines, I should mention that this one was actually prompted by a fantastic Pavillon Blanc, a white Bordeaux. The coconut milk provides softness, the poppy seeds are thought to be an aphrodisiac, the ginger adds heat, and the lemon grass cools—all counterpoints for the complexity of the wine. This is not for calorie-counters, just for diners who love great taste!

1. Heat the oil in a large heavy-bottomed saucepan over medium heat. Add the shallots and sauté for about 3 minutes, or until the shallots have wilted and begun to take on some color. Stir in the cilantro, ginger, poppy seeds, cloves, cinnamon, turmeric, and lemongrass. Sauté for 5 minutes, lowering the heat, if necessary, to keep the mixture from burning.

2. Add the lobster and continue sautéing for an additional 3 minutes. Stir in the coconut milk and bring to a simmer. Allow to just barely simmer for 5 minutes.

3. Stir in the cream and bring to a boil. Immediately lower the heat and gently simmer for about 15 minutes, or until the flavors are well blended and the soup has reduced slightly. Taste and adjust seasoning with salt, if necessary.

4. Pour an equal portion into each of 6 shallow soup bowls and serve immediately.

Carrot-Saffron Soup

12 medium carrots, peeled and sliced
8 cups water
1 tablespoon saffron powder
Coarse salt, to taste
1 tablespoon saffron threads
  (optional)

To me, carrot juice is the essence of good health in a glass, so I have tried to translate this fresh pure taste into a soup. What could be simpler to cook than carrots and water? Add a hint of saffron for complex flavor without complex cooking. This is a delicious light soup that is good hot or cold and also makes a great base for a vegetable sorbet.

1. Put the carrots and water in a large saucepan over high heat. Bring to a boil. Lower the heat and simmer for 10 minutes, or until the carrots are very tender. Drain, reserving the cooking water.

2. Put the carrots in a blender and puree, adding the cooking water 1 cup at a time, until the puree has a souplike consistency. You may have to do this in batches. Add the saffron powder and salt and process just to blend.

3. Pour the soup into a clean saucepan and place over medium heat. Bring to a simmer. Remove from the heat and pour an equal portion into each of 6 shallow soup bowls. Serve hot, sprinkled with some saffron threads, if desired.

Note: To serve the soup chilled, do not reheat after blending. Place in a nonreactive container, cover, and refrigerate for at least 4 hours, until well chilled.

To use as a sorbet, chill as above and then process in an ice cream maker according to the manufacturer's directions.

Chilled Cucumber Soup
with Dill and Mustard Seeds

Serves 6

2 tablespoons canola oil

1/4 teaspoon mustard seeds

2 large cucumbers

4 cups buttermilk

1/4 cup chopped fresh dill

Coarse salt, to taste

When I first met Lou, my fiancé, his pantry was devoid of spices (and food!). Since he is very health conscious, I began adding spices to his kitchen so that when I cooked there, I could add zest to the light dishes he desired. This is one of his favorites. The best thing about it? It tastes better the next day! Since it is easy to double the quantity, it is a perfect summertime, weekend-guests-expected soup. It has its roots in a classic Indian *raita*; can you tell?

1. Heat the oil in a small sauté pan over medium heat. Add the mustard seeds and sauté for about 2 minutes, or until the seeds begin to take on some color and are very aromatic. Remove from the heat and allow to cool.

2. Peel and seed the cucumbers. Cut into 1/4-inch dice and place in a large nonreactive container. Stir in the buttermilk, dill, and salt.

3. Stir the mustard seeds into the cucumber mixture. Cover and refrigerate for at least 4 hours, until chilled.

4. When ready to serve, pour an equal portion into each of 6 shallow soup bowls and serve.

Velouté of Curried Butternut Squash Soup

Serves 6

1 large butternut squash
2 tablespoons canola oil
1 tablespoon coarse salt, plus more to taste
4 cups water
1 tablespoon Curry Spice Blend (see page 14) or curry powder
1/4 teaspoon freshly ground pepper

In India during the monsoon season (late summer, early winter), squash is everywhere, and it is not uncommon to find it used in everything from soup to dessert. If you are entertaining, you can use frozen squash puree for a quick and easy first course, but you might need to add a pinch of brown sugar to heighten the sweetness of the processed squash. I have also used this soup as a sauce for quail and *poussin* with great success.

1. Preheat the oven to 450°F.
2. Prick the squash with a fork in a number of spots to allow any steam to escape while baking. Rub with the oil and 1 tablespoon of salt. Place on a small baking sheet in the preheated oven and bake for about 45 minutes, or until very tender when pierced with a knife point. Remove from the oven and allow to set until cool enough to handle.
3. When the squash is cool enough to handle-cut in half lengthwise and carefully remove the seeds. Scrape the pulp from the skin.
4. Put the squash pulp in a blender and begin processing. With the blender running, add enough of the water to make a light consommé. Blend in the curry powder, pepper, and salt to taste.
5. Pour the consommé into a medium saucepan and bring to a boil over medium-high heat. Lower the heat and simmer for 5 minutes. Pour an equal portion into each of 6 consommé cups and serve very hot.

Tamarind Consommé

Serves 6

Pinch ground asafetida

1 teaspoon ghee (see page 15)

2 tablespoons peanut oil

$1/4$ teaspoon mustard seeds

$1/4$ teaspoon cumin seeds

$1/4$ teaspoon dark, toasted ground fenugreek

$1/4$ teaspoon ground turmeric

$1/4$ cup tamarind pulp (see page 18)

2 tablespoons jaggery (see page18)

15 fresh curry leaves

2 quarts water

Coarse salt, to taste

Tamarind soup is a staple in every South Indian home. My grand-mother would make it to get our appetites going. Here I've used the classic French idea of a clean, clear broth to initiate a rich meal, but the taste and aroma I've created are definitely from the East. I find it a mysterious and inviting way to engage my guests. Thank you, Grandmom!

1. Combine the asafetida and ghee in a small sauté pan over medium heat. Cook, stirring frequently, for about 2 minutes, or until the asafetida is lightly toasted. Remove from the heat.
2. Heat the oil in a large saucepan over medium-high heat. Add the mustard and cumin seeds and sauté for 3 minutes. Add the fenugreek, turmeric, and reserved asafetida mixture and sauté for an additional minute.
3. Stir in the tamarind, jaggery, and curry leaves. Add the water and salt. Raise the heat and bring the mixture to a boil. Lower the heat and simmer for 10 minutes. Strain through a fine strainer into a clean saucepan. Return to medium heat and bring to a boil. Remove from the heat.
4. Pour an equal portion into each of 6 consommé cups and serve hot.

Salads and Side Dishes

Salads

Carpaccio of Cured Beef with Baby Greens and Mung Bean Polenta

Lobster Tail with Red and Yellow Pepper Coulis and Potato Roulade

Crostini of Salmon with Lemon-Leek Sauce

Pan-Seared Scallops with Garlic-Scented Zucchini

Corn Compote in a Pappadam Bowl

Side Dishes

Snap Beans with Coriander-Coconut Crust

Savory Spinach Gratin

Fava Bean Puree Seasoned with Hot Spices

Indian Spiced Ratatouille

Potato Gratin with Onions, Garlic, and Saffron

Spiced Basmati Rice with Fruit and Nuts

Carpaccio of Cured Beef
with Baby Greens and Mung Bean Polenta

1 cup split mung beans

³/₄ cup olive oil

1 teaspoon ground cayenne

1 teaspoon ground coriander

1 teaspoon ground cumin

Pinch of ground turmeric

One ³/₄-pound piece prime beef
    tenderloin, fat removed

¹/₄ cup sun-dried tomatoes

¹/₄ cup dry white wine

Coarse salt and freshly ground black
    pepper, to taste

¹/₄ teaspoon ajowan

¹/₄ cup ghee (see page 15)

¹/₂ pound mixed baby salad greens,
    well washed and dried

¹/₄ cup ¹/₄-inch dice carrots, blanched
    (optional)

¹/₄ cup ¹/₄-inch dice zucchini,
    blanched (optional)

¹/₄ cup ¹/₄-inch dice yellow squash,
    blanched (optional)

I don't usually venture outside of Indian and French cuisine, but I think the light Italian touches of carpaccio and sun-dried tomato provide a perfect backdrop for the other ingredients in the dish. This recipe requires the finest quality beef, preferably dry-aged, with beautiful marbling. Like many of today's chefs, I take some liberties with culinary terms. Here I call the mung bean puree polenta, because that is how it seems to me in the recipe. Though the dish has many components, much of the work can be done ahead of time.

1. Place the mung beans in a medium bowl with cold water to cover by at least 2 inches. Allow to soak for 8 hours.

2. Combine ¹/₄ cup of the olive oil with the cayenne, coriander, cumin, and turmeric in a small bowl. When well blended, rub the mixture onto the beef. Place on a glass dish and refrigerate, uncovered, for 4 hours.

3. Place the sun-dried tomatoes in a heat-proof container and cover with boiling water. Allow to soak for about 10 minutes, or until the tomatoes have plumped slightly. Drain well.

4. To make the vinaigrette, combine the tomatoes with the wine and remaining olive oil in a blender. Process until smooth. Taste and adjust seasoning with salt and pepper. Set aside.

5. Preheat the oven to 400°F.

6. Drain the mung beans, reserving the soaking water. Place the beans in a blender and, with the motor running, add enough of

the reserved soaking water to make a smooth, thick puree. Add the *ajowan* and salt to taste and process to blend.

7. Pour the mung bean puree into a nonstick 9-inch round pie plate, smoothing out the top with a wet spatula. Bake for 10 minutes, or until the bean polenta is firm and beginning to take on some color. Remove from the oven and cover to keep warm.

8. Remove the beef from the refrigerator and season with salt. Using a very sharp knife cut crosswise into 24 paper-thin slices.

9. Using a 3-inch round pastry cutter, cut 6 circles of equal size from the warm polenta. Place a circle on each of 6 luncheon plates. Place 4 slices of beef carpaccio, slightly overlapping, over the circle. Sprinkle the baby greens on top of the carpaccio; then, if desired, sprinkle equal portions of the diced vegetables around the plate. Drizzle the vinaigrette over all and serve.

Note: The mung bean puree can be cooked early in the day. The polenta circles can be cut and wrapped in aluminum foil, and reheated just before serving.

Wine Suggestions: Maître d'Estournel
BV Rutherford Cabernet Sauvignon
Cabernet-Merlot blend will stand up well to the beef and the harshness of the greens.

Lobster Tail with Red and Yellow Pepper Coulis and Potato Roulade

Serves 6

3 red bell peppers

3 yellow bell peppers

4 tablespoons olive oil

6 fresh curry leaves

Coarse salt, to taste

2 large Yukon gold potatoes, peeled and cut into 1/2-inch dice

2 carrots, peeled, trimmed, and cut into 1/4-inch dice

1 tablespoon peanut oil

$\frac{1}{2}$ cup finely chopped onion

1 teaspoon minced fresh ginger

$\frac{1}{4}$ cup fresh peas

$\frac{1}{4}$ teaspoon ground cloves

$\frac{1}{4}$ teaspoon ground cinnamon

Pinch of ground turmeric

$\frac{1}{2}$ cup water

3 tablespoons ghee (see page 15)

$\frac{1}{2}$ teaspoon saffron threads

6 lobster tails, shells removed (see Note)

6 sprigs fresh cilantro

Although this is not a dish to prepare every day, it certainly deserves a place on the table for special occasions. The potato roulade is based on a typical South Indian potato curry, but I've "sanitized" it a bit so that it would not inflame the lobster. The beauty of this presentation is in the intense colors of the pepper coulis, which serve as the background for the delicate but robustly flavored roulade and lobster. The contrasting textures and aromatic flavors combine to make a spectacular plate. Much of the preparation can be done in advance, so that the last minute work is minimal.

1. Preheat the oven to 400°F.

2. Place the peppers on a low-sided baking sheet. Roast in the oven for 45 minutes, turning occasionally, or until the peppers are very soft and the skin is nicely charred. Remove from the oven and place the red peppers in one plastic bag and yellow peppers in another. Seal the bags and allow the peppers to steam for about 10 minutes. Remove the peppers from the bags and, using your fingertips, gently peel the charred skin from each pepper. Carefully cut the peppers in half and remove and discard the stem, seeds, and membrane.

3. Place the yellow peppers in a blender with 2 tablespoons of the olive oil and 3 curry leaves and process until smooth. Season with salt. Pour into a nonreactive container and set aside.

4. Place the red peppers in a clean blender with the remaining 2

tablespoons of olive oil and 3 curry leaves and process until smooth. Season with salt. Pour into a nonreactive container and set aside.

5. Put the potatoes, and cold salted water to cover, in a medium saucepan over medium-high heat. Bring to a boil. Lower the heat and simmer for about 10 minutes, or until the potatoes are tender but still firm. Drain well and pat dry. Set aside.

6. Put the carrots, and cold salted water to cover, in a small saucepan over medium-high heat. Bring to a boil. Lower the heat and simmer for about 5 minutes or until the carrots are tender but still firm. Drain well and pat dry. Set aside.

7. Heat the peanut oil in a large nonstick sauté pan over medium heat. Add the onion and sauté for 7 minutes, or until soft. Stir in the ginger and continue to sauté for another 2 minutes, lowering the heat if necessary to keep the onion from browning.

8. Stir in the reserved potatoes and carrots. Add the peas, cloves, cinnamon, and turmeric. When well combined, add the water and stir. Cook for 10 minutes, or until the mixture has thickened and the flavors are well blended. Taste and adjust seasoning with salt. Remove from the heat and allow to cool slightly.

9. Combine the ghee and saffron. Generously coat the lobster tails with the ghee mixture. Season with salt.

10. Place a cast-iron skillet over high heat. When very hot but not smoking, add the lobster tails and sear each side for about 2 minutes, or until lobster is just cooked.

11. Spoon some of the reserved yellow pepper coulis on one side and an equal amount of the reserved red pepper coulis on the other side of each of 6 luncheon plates.

12. Firmly pack an equal portion of the potato mixture to come about halfway up the sides of six 3-inch pastry rings. Carefully place a ring into the center of each plate, gently lifting it up with one hand as you force the potato roulade down into the center of the plate. Place a warm lobster tail on top of each potato roulade. Garnish with a cilantro sprig and serve.

Note: I always buy whole lobsters and use every bit for salads, sauces, stocks, or garnishes. When I make this recipe, I often use the head to garnish the plate. (See photo opposite.)

Wine Suggestions: Pavillon Blanc
Voss Sauvignon Blanc
Both of these wine selections are loaded with a delicate acidity that nicely complements the rich, sweet flavors of this dish.

Crostini of Salmon
with Lemon-Leek Sauce

Serves 6

2 teaspoons ghee (see page 15)

1 cup finely chopped leeks, white part
only

$1/2$ fresh jalapeño chile, stemmed,
seeded, and minced

1 cup heavy cream

Coarse salt, to taste

3 tablespoons fresh lemon juice

2 large Idaho potatoes, peeled

12 large fresh spinach leaves,
stemmed

$3/4$ pound boneless, skinless salmon
fillet, cut into six pieces

6 cups vegetable oil (approximately)

3 cups julienned fresh spinach

I find salmon served as a first course to be quite rare (with the exception of smoked salmon), so I decided to add some to my menu. More exotic than a piece of grilled salmon, this crostini recipe is one of my most requested dishes. It does require a Japanese vegetable turner, as there is no other device that can create the fine potato strands that are necessary to complete the dish. This simple tool is a small investment that will enhance your creativity in the kitchen.

1. Heat the ghee in a medium sauté pan over medium heat. Add the leeks and jalapeño and sauté for about 5 minutes, or until the leeks are very soft but not brown.

2. Stir in the cream. Add salt and bring to a simmer. Lower the heat and barely simmer for about 15 minutes, or until the cream has reduced by one half. Remove from the heat and whisk in the lemon juice. Pour through a fine strainer into the top half of a double boiler sitting over very hot water and keep the sauce warm.

3. Using a Japanese vegetable turner, cut the potatoes into long strands. Lightly season with salt and set aside.

4. Working quickly, wrap 2 spinach leaves around each piece of salmon. Immediately wrap equal portions of potato strands around each spinach-wrapped salmon piece, pushing firmly with your hands to secure the packet.

5. Heat the oil in a deep-fat fryer to 360°F.

6. When the oil is hot, add the salmon pieces and fry for about

3 minutes, or until the potatoes are golden and crisp. Using a slotted spoon, remove the salmon packets from the oil and allow to drain on paper towels.

7. Spoon about 2 tablespoons of the warm sauce onto each of 6 luncheon plates. Place a mound of julienned spinach in the center. Next place a salmon crostini in the center of the spinach and serve.

Note: The potato-wrapped salmon crostini can be made early in the day and stored in the refrigerator, tightly wrapped in plastic film.

Wine Suggestions: Kistler Sonoma Coast Chardonnay
Bouchard Puligny-Montrachet
A big, buttery, rich Chardonnay is the complementary match for this flavorful salad.

Pan-Seared Scallops
with Garlic-Scented Zucchini

Serves 6

1 tablespoon peanut oil

2 medium zucchini, trimmed and chopped

$^1/_2$ jalapeño chile, stemmed, seeded, and minced

$^1/_4$ teaspoon minced garlic

$^1/_4$ teaspoon crushed ajowan

1 teaspoon coarse salt (approximately), plus more to taste

Pinch of sugar

24 medium scallops

6 tablespoons ghee (see page 15)

6 sprigs fresh sage (optional)

This recipe was the benchmark that told me I was confident about my culinary combinations. The *ajowan* has a very distinct perfume and sharp taste that heightens the delicacy of the scallops and the blandness of the zucchini. It is most important not to overcook the zucchini, so that it remains as green as possible, brightening the plate and accenting the scallops.

1. Heat the oil in a medium sauté pan over medium heat. Add the zucchini, jalapeño, garlic, and *ajowan* and sauté for about 4 minutes, or until the zucchini is slightly soft but remains bright green. Remove from the heat and cool the mixture slightly.
2. Place in a food processor fitted with the metal blade and process to a very thick and smooth texture. (It should be almost as thick as wasabi). Taste and adjust the seasoning with salt.
3. Combine 1 teaspoon salt with the sugar and season the scallops with the mixture. Rub each scallop with a bit of ghee.
4. Heat the remaining ghee in a large sauté pan over high heat. Add the scallops and sear for about 3 minutes, or until the scallops are golden and just cooked through.
5. Place an equal portion of the zucchini in the center of each of 6 warm luncheon plates. Push 4 scallops into the zucchini on each plate and serve, garnished with a sprig of sage, if desired.

Wine Suggestion: Cakebread Sauvignon Blanc
The herbaceousness of the Sauvignon grape matches well with this delicate scallop dish.

Corn Compote in a Pappadam Bowl

Serves 6

$^1/_4$ cup fresh curry leaves

$^1/_4$ cup balsamic vinegar

$^1/_2$ cup plus 1 tablespoon olive oil

Coarse salt, to taste

2 cups vegetable oil (approximately)

6 pappadams (see Note)

4 cups fresh corn kernels or frozen
   kernels, thawed and well drained

$^1/_4$ cup diced red pepper

$^1/_4$ cup diced red onion

$^1/_2$ teaspoon Curry Spice Blend (see
   page 15) or curry powder

$^1/_4$ teaspoon minced garlic

3 tablespoons fresh lime juice

1 cup mung bean sprouts

6 cups mixed baby salad greens

I adore pappadams—they were on our table every day through-out my childhood. When I first opened my restaurant, every time I looked at a package of pappadams, I wondered whether there was something more I could do with them, other than place them on the table as bread. Since then, inspiration has run wild, and I have used them for napoleons, elaborate garnishes, plates, and, as in this recipe, for bowls. And I'm sure that I've yet to exhaust their possibilities.

1. Place the curry leaves and the balsamic vinegar in a blender and process until quite smooth. With the motor running, slowly add $^1/_2$ cup of the olive oil, blending until well emulsified. Taste and adjust seasoning with salt. Set the vinaigrette aside.

2. Heat the vegetable oil in a pan large enough to hold 1 pappadam allowing enough oil so that it will cover the pappadam. When the oil is very hot but not smoking, fry 1 pappadam at a time, removing it from the oil when it is lightly browned but still pliable. Immediately fit it into a larger bowl and place a smaller one on top of it to mold the pappadam into a bowl shape. Carefully remove the pappadam "bowl" from the mold and set aside. Continue making pappadam bowls in this manner until you have 6.

3. Heat the remaining tablespoon of olive oil in a medium sauté pan over medium heat. Add the corn kernels, curry powder, garlic, and salt to taste. Sauté for about 4 minutes, or until corn is just slightly cooked. Stir in the lime juice and remove from the heat. Allow to cool slightly.

4. Toss in the mung bean sprouts.

5. Put the salad greens in a mixing bowl. Drizzle with the reserved vinaigrette and toss to combine.

6. Place a pappadam bowl in the center of each of 6 luncheon plates. Spoon equal portions of the corn mixture into the bowls. Mound equal portions of the dressed salad greens on top of the corn mixture and serve.

Note: A pappadam is a wafer-thin Indian flat bread made with lentil flour. It is available from East Indian, Pakistani, or Middle Eastern markets, some specialty food stores, or by mail order from one of the sources listed on page 209.

You will need two bowls, one slightly larger than the other, to serve as a mold, as well as a fast hand to turn the hot, quick-to-crisp pappadam into a bowl shape. I use this two-bowl method as it seems to help the pappadam mold into a firm shape. I suggest that you have a few extra pappadams with which you can practice the technique. Your efforts will be rewarded with edible bowls for a light salad.

You can use frozen corn kernels, but they should be very well drained of water before cooking.

Wine Suggestions: Georges Duboeuf Viognier
Pine Ridge Chenin Blanc
Either of these delicate, slightly sweet wines would partner well with this crunchy, lightly spiced vegetable compote.

Snap Beans
with Coriander-Coconut Crust

Serves 6

¹/₄ cup *chana dal* (see page 32)

3 tablespoons toasted split coriander dal (see Note)

¹/₂ teaspoon ground cayenne

¹/₄ teaspoon cumin seeds

4 whole cloves

One 2-inch cinnamon stick

Coarse salt to taste

6 tablespoons ghee (see page 15)

1 pound green beans, trimmed, washed, and dried

1 cup fresh coconut puree (see Note)

This is a very Indian side dish, heady with spices and sweet with coconut. When I was growing up, we had these beans at least once a week with a big bowl of fragrant rice. The beans are an excellent accompaniment to pork, chicken, or grilled fish.

1. Put the *chana dal*, coriander dal, cayenne, cumin, cloves, and cinnamon in a small sauté pan over medium heat. Sauté for about 3 minutes, or until the spices are golden brown and very aromatic. Stir in salt along with 1 tablespoon of ghee. Remove from the heat and set aside.

2. Heat the remaining ghee in a large sauté pan over medium heat. Add the beans, coconut puree, and the reserved spice mixture. Sauté for about 15 minutes, or until the beans are tender and the sauce has thickened. Remove from the heat and serve hot.

Note: Chana dal *and split coriander dal are available at Indian, Pakistani, or Middle Eastern markets, at some specialty food stores, or through one of the mail order sources listed on page 209.*

Fresh coconut puree is made by placing fresh coconut, peeled of all its brown skin, in a blender with a bit of water and processing until smooth.

Wine Suggestions: Remy Pannier Vouvray
Lindemans Bin 65 Chardonnay
Either of these wines have the high degree of fruitiness required to meet the natural sweetness of the coconut.

Savory Spinach Gratin

1 teaspoon olive oil

2 pounds fresh spinach, well washed, dried, and stemmed

1 teaspoon minced fresh dill

$1/2$ teaspoon minced garlic

$1/2$ teaspoon Curry Spice Blend (page 14) or curry powder

$1/4$ teaspoon toasted ground cumin

Coarse salt and freshly ground black pepper, to taste

$1 1/2$ cups fresh bread crumbs

$1/4$ cup ghee (see page 15)

This simple gratin, based on a traditional French recipe, makes a wonderful side dish for pork or chicken. If fresh spinach is unavailable, use 2 packages frozen chopped spinach. Just make sure that you thaw and drain it very well before proceeding with the recipe. Curry powder embraces and softens the sometimes mineral taste of spinach.

1. Preheat the oven to 400°F.
2. Lightly grease a 9-inch gratin dish with the olive oil.
3. Coarsely chop the spinach, and in a large bowl, toss it with the dill, garlic, curry powder, cumin, salt, and pepper. When well combined, firmly pack the mixture into the prepared gratin dish. Sprinkle the bread crumbs generously on top. Drizzle the ghee over the crumbs, making sure they are well coated.
4. Bake the gratin for about 45 minutes, or until the spinach liquid has evaporated and the top has browned. Remove from the oven and serve immediately.

Wine Suggestions: Château Ste.-Michèle Gewürztraminer
Zaca Mesa Roussann
These delicate white wines enhance the slightly spiced leafiness of the spinach gratin.

Fava Bean Puree
Seasoned with Hot Spices

Serves 6

6 pounds fresh fava beans, shelled
  and peeled
1/2 jalapeño chile, stemmed and
  seeded
1 cup chopped onion
1/4 teaspoon minced garlic
3 tablespoons ghee (see page 15)
1 teaspoon Garam Masala (see
  page 14)
Coarse salt and freshly ground black
  pepper, to taste

For this recipe, you can use fresh fava beans that are a bit old because you want some starchiness to thicken the puree. However, they should still be a lively green color, rather than yellowish. The sweet spices in the garam masala definitely add an intriguing note, without overwhelming the beans. This is an excellent dish for almost any roasted or grilled meat or poultry.

1. Put the beans, chile, onion, and garlic in a medium saucepan with boiling, salted water to cover. Bring to a boil, lower the heat, and simmer for about 15 minutes, or until the beans are very tender. Drain through a fine sieve placed over a bowl, reserving the cooking liquid.
2. Put the bean mixture in a food processor fitted with the metal blade and begin to process to a very thick puree, adding some of the reserved cooking liquid if necessary.
3. Scrape the puree into a medium nonstick saucepan. Place over medium-low heat and beat in the ghee and garam masala. Cook, stirring constantly, for about 3 minutes, or until the mixture is well blended and very hot. Taste and adjust seasoning with salt and pepper. Serve immediately.

Wine Suggestions: Bonny Doon Pacific Rim Riesling
Trefethen Riesling
The sweet acidity of the Riesling grape offsets the mellow spiciness of this bean puree.

Indian Spiced Ratatouille

Serves 6

2 small eggplants
1 tablespoon coarse salt, plus more to
    taste
$1/4$ cup olive oil
1 teaspoon black mustard seeds
$1/2$ teaspoon cumin seeds
Pinch of ground asafetida
4 cups chopped onions
4 cloves garlic, peeled and sliced
$1/2$ jalapeño chile, stemmed, seeded,
    and chopped
10 fresh curry leaves, chopped
$1 1/2$ pounds very ripe tomatoes,
    peeled, cored, seeded, and
    chopped
2 red bell peppers, cored, seeded,
    and cubed
2 green bell peppers, cored, seeded,
    and cubed
Freshly ground black pepper, to taste
$1 1/2$ cups diced zucchini
$1/4$ cup chopped fresh cilantro

This has all of the ingredients of a classic Provençal ratatouille, with the added zest of some traditional Indian spices. I find it interesting that the common vegetables of the South of France are the same everyday vegetables of my South Indian childhood. This is an excellent summer side dish to serve with grilled meats or fish; it can also be used as a first course, with grilled peasant bread or one of the Indian flat breads as an accompaniment.

1. Stem and cube the eggplants; leave the peel on. Toss the cubes with the coarse salt. Put them in a colander in a sink to drain for 30 minutes. Rinse off the excess salt and pat dry. Set aside.
2. Heat the oil in a large saucepan over medium heat. Add the mustard and cumin seeds and cook, stirring constantly, for about 1 minute, or until the seeds begin to pop. Add the asafetida and stir to combine.
3. Add the onions, garlic, chile, and curry leaves and sauté for about 10 minutes, or until the vegetables begin to color. Immediately add the eggplant and continue to cook for 10 minutes.
4. Stir in the tomatoes and peppers. Season with salt and pepper. Lower the heat and gently simmer for 15 minutes.
5. Stir in the zucchini and continue to cook, stirring frequently, for an additional 30 minutes. Taste again and adjust the seasonings. If the mixture still has quite a bit of liquid, spoon off some of the excess so that you have a thick vegetable mélange.

6. Remove from the heat and stir in the cilantro. Allow the ratatouille to cool to room temperature before serving.

Wine Suggestions: Castello Banfi Chianti Classico
Ravenswood Vintner's Blend Zinfandel
This Indian ratatouille absolutely demands a peppery, spicy red wine such as the Chianti or Zinfandel that we have chosen.

Potato Gratin
with Onions, Garlic, and Saffron

Serves 6

1 cup heavy cream

1 teaspoon crumbled saffron threads

3 tablespoons ghee (see page 15)

3 pounds Yukon gold potatoes,
  peeled and thinly sliced

1 large onion, peeled and thinly sliced

1 tablespoon minced garlic

Coarse salt and freshly ground black
  pepper, to taste

$^1/_4$ teaspoon ground nutmeg

Potatoes, nutmeg, and garam masala are a classic Indian combination. Here, a traditional French gratin is livened up with a bit of saffron and nutmeg. It is an excellent side dish for any roasted or grilled meat. With the addition of some grated cheese, it would also make a great luncheon main course.

1. Combine the heavy cream and saffron in a small saucepan over medium heat. Bring to a simmer. Remove immediately from the heat and allow to set for 30 minutes.

2. In the meantime, preheat the oven to 350°F.

3. Using some of the ghee, generously grease a 9-inch gratin dish. Set aside.

4. Put the potatoes, onion, and garlic in a large saucepan filled with cold, salted water to barely cover. Bring to a boil over high heat and cook for 3 minutes. Drain well and pat dry.

5. Combine the potato mixture with the remaining ghee and the salt and pepper in the prepared gratin dish and smooth the top with a spatula. Pour the saffron cream over the top, and sprinkle with a bit of nutmeg.

6. Bake for about 1 hour, or until the potatoes are meltingly tender and the top is golden. If the top begins to brown too quickly, reduce the heat, as it is important that the potatoes become extremely tender.

7. Let stand for about 5 minutes and cut into wedges.

Wine Suggestions: Cambria Katherine's Chardonnay
Louis Latour Meursault

Spiced Basmati Rice
with Fruit and Pine Nuts

Serves 6

3 tablespoons ghee (see page 15)

$^1/_2$ cup finely minced onion

1 teaspoon minced fresh ginger

$^1/_2$ teaspoon minced fresh garlic

3 whole cloves

3 cardamom pods

One 2-inch cinnamon stick

2 cups basmati rice, rinsed and
   drained

1 teaspoon ground turmeric

2 $^1/_2$ cups water

$^1/_2$ cup coconut milk (see page 18)

Coarse salt, to taste

$^1/_4$ cup golden raisins

$^1/_4$ cup finely diced dried apricots

$^1/_2$ cup toasted pine nuts

This classic and very rich rice dish can be served with almost any meat or poultry. Traditionally, the whole spices are left in the dish when the rice is served, but they are never eaten.

1. Heat the ghee in a heavy-bottomed medium saucepan over medium heat. Add the onion, ginger, garlic, cloves, cardamom pods, and cinnamon stick and sauté for 5 minutes. Stir in the rice and turmeric and continue to sauté for about 3 minutes, or until the rice is shiny.

2. Raise the heat and add the water, coconut milk, and salt. Bring to a boil. Immediately reduce the heat to low and cover the saucepan. Cook for 10 minutes; then stir in the raisins and apricots. Cover again and cook, without lifting the lid, for 10 more minutes.

3. Remove the pan from the heat and, without lifting the lid, allow the rice to steam for 5 minutes.

4. Remove the lid and stir in the pine nuts. Remove the whole spices if you wish before serving.

Note: For a sweet dessert rice, eliminate the onions and garlic and add about $^1/_4$ cup of jaggery (page 18) when you add the water and coconut milk.

Wine Suggestions: Rosemount Syrah
Qupé Syrah
The rich fruitiness of the spiced rice calls for an equally fruity grape such as the Syrah to bring it to full measure.

Meat

Tenderloin of Pork with Black Mustard Rub, Collard Greens, and Curried Blueberry Sauce

South Indian Barbecue with Collard Greens and Black-Eyed Peas

Filet of Beef with Butternut Squash Consommé

Buffalo Rib-Eye with Black Pepper and Coriander Crust and Cranberry Coulis

Cassoulet of Veal with Tempered Lentils and Provençal Herbs

Veal Medallions Wrapped in Lotus Leaf

Roasted Leg of Lamb with Mint Chutney and Mint-Flavored Potatoes

Baby Lamb Racks with Curry Leaf–Black Pepper Crust and Curried Blackberry Sauce

Lamb Stew with Vindaloo Spices and Sweet Squash and Turnips

Tenderloin of Pork
with Black Mustard Rub, Collard Greens,
and Curried Blueberry Sauce

Serves 6

¹/₄ cup wildflower honey

3 tablespoons Dijon mustard

1 tablespoon fresh rosemary leaves, crushed

1 tablespoon mustard seeds

1 tablespoon cracked black pepper

Coarse salt, to taste

1 ¹/₂ tablespoons black mustard seeds

6 tablespoons olive oil

Two 1 ¹/₂-pound pork tenderloins, well trimmed of fat and silverskin removed

1 large bunch collard greens, well washed and dried

1 pint blueberries, well washed, picked over, and patted dry (see Note)

¹/₄ teaspoon Curry Spice Blend (page 14) or curry powder

¹/₈ teaspoon toasted ground fenugreek

Tabasco, to taste

1 tablespoon canola oil

1 tablespoon ghee (see page 15)

Curried Blueberry Sauce? I promise this was not done for the shock value. The sauce is the perfect complement to tenderloin of pork, one of my favorite meats. Because it does not have a strong taste or dense texture, the tenderloin readily absorbs many of the aromatic spices that I enjoy. Although pork is not eaten in India, I, personally, do not have any objections to it.

1. Combine the honey, mustard, rosemary, mustard seeds, pepper, and salt with 1 tablespoon of the black mustard seeds in a nonreactive shallow dish large enough to hold the pork. Blend in 2 tablespoons of the olive oil. Lay the pork in the dish, turning to coat all over with the marinade. Cover with plastic film and refrigerate for 4 hours, turning the pork occasionally.

2. Cut the ribs from the collard greens. Working with about 6 leaves at a time, stack them, one on top of the other, and then roll them up, cigar fashion. Cut each roll, crosswise, into ¹/₄-inch pieces. (These ragged strips are called a "chiffonade".) When all of the greens have been cut into chiffonade, place them in a medium saucepan filled with rapidly boiling salted water, for about 3 minutes, or until just tender. Drain in a sieve and immediately refresh under cold, running water. Using a paper towel, pat the greens dry. Set aside.

3. Preheat the oven to 350°F.

4. Put the blueberries, curry powder, and fenugreek in a blender. Add the remaining olive oil and puree until well combined, but not smooth. Taste and adjust seasoning with salt

and Tabasco. Transfer to a small nonreactive saucepan over low heat and cook for about 5 minutes, or just until flavors have blended. Cover and set aside on the stovetop to keep warm.

5. Pour the canola oil into a large nonstick, ovenproof sauté pan over high heat. When hot, but not smoking, add the pork and sear, turning frequently, for about 3 minutes, or until the outside is nicely browned. Transfer the pan immediately to the oven and roast the pork, turning occasionally, for about 12 minutes or until an instant-read thermometer reaches 140°F. when inserted into the thickest part of the tenderloin. The pork should be cooked through, but still pink in the center. Remove from the oven and allow the pork to rest for a couple of minutes to seal in the juices.

6. Heat the ghee in a large nonstick sauté pan over medium-high heat. Add the collard chiffonade and sauté for about 3 minutes, or until the collards deepen in color.

7. Place a large shallow circle of the blueberry sauce over the bottom of each of 6 dinner plates. Using tongs, place a loosely stacked pile of collard chiffonade in the center. Cut the pork, crosswise, into 2-inch-thick pieces and place two pieces, leaning against one another, into the collards. Sprinkle a few of the remaining black mustard seeds over each plate and serve.

Note: Fresh blueberries may be replaced with high-quality frozen blueberries.

Wine Suggestions: Markham Merlot
Moueix Merlot
The fleshy berry-and-spice traits of the Merlot grape pair beautifully with this dish.

South Indian Barbecue
with Collard Greens and Black-Eyed Peas

Serves 6

3 cups fresh shelled black-eyed peas
6 cups cold water
1 6-ounce jar commercially prepared
  Indian mango pickle, preferably
  with garlic (see Note)
$^1/_2$ cup olive oil
4 cloves garlic (optional)
Coarse salt, to taste
6 pounds pork short ribs
$^1/_2$ teaspoon ground cayenne
$^1/_2$ teaspoon ground cumin
6 tablespoons peanut oil
6 cups chopped fresh collard greens
$^1/_2$ cup dry white wine

This recipe began as a joke. One evening, a regular customer called to see if we had any tables open for dinner. After I assured him of his favorite spot, he went on to say that he was having a difficult time deciding whether to eat at Raji's or hunt up some great barbecue. Since he opted for Raji's, I created this especially for him, so that he could have the best of both worlds. That night, the barbecue went on the staff menu, and with the staff's endorsement, it has stayed, in one form or another, on the restaurant menu.

1. Combine the black-eyed peas and water in a medium saucepan over high heat. Bring to a boil. Lower the heat and simmer for 10 minutes, or until the peas are tender. Drain well and set aside.

2. Spoon the mango pickle into a fine sieve and drain well. Check to make sure that there are no shells or woody pieces of mango. If there are, discard and replace with clean pieces. Place the pickle in a blender. Add the olive oil and, if garlic is not already in the pickle, the optional garlic and process to a smooth puree. Add salt and set aside.

3. Preheat the oven to 300°F.

4. Cut the pork into ribs. Wash them in cold running water and pat dry. Rub the ribs with the mango pickle puree. Place on a rack in a large roasting pan and roast for 2 hours, or until so tender that the meat almost falls off the bone.

5. About 15 minutes before the ribs are done, prepare the peas

and collards. Combine the cooked black-eyed peas with the cayenne, cumin, 3 tablespoons of the peanut oil, and salt to taste in a medium saucepan. Cook over medium heat, stirring frequently, for about 10 minutes, or until the flavors are well blended. If the peas begin to dry out during cooking time add up to ½ cup of water.

6. Pour the remaining peanut oil in a large sauté pan over medium heat. Add the collards and salt to taste and sauté for about 5 minutes, or until the collards are just wilted and beginning to cook.

7. Remove the ribs from the roasting pan. Drain off any excess fat. Place the roasting pan on a burner on top of the stove over high heat. Add the wine and bring to boil. Remove from the heat.

8. Divide the ribs among 6 dinner plates, reserving 1 additional rib for each plate. Spoon an equal portion of black-eyed peas and then collards on top of the ribs. Prop a reserved rib into the greens on each plate. Drizzle the pan sauce around the plate and serve.

Note: I use commercially prepared Indian mango pickle, as homemade takes quite a few weeks to mature. The commercial pickle has already had time to absorb the spices and acidity that make it such an integral part of the Indian table.

Wine Suggestions: Franciscan Magnificant
Hess Collection Cabernet Sauvignon
A Cabernet-based wine brilliantly enhances the flavors of this unique barbecue.

Filet of Beef
with Butternut Squash Consommé

Serves 6

1 large butternut squash
2 large carrots, peeled and julienned
2 teaspoons freshly ground black pepper
1 teaspoon Curry Spice Blend (page 14) or curry powder
1 teaspoon ground allspice
Coarse salt, to taste
4 cups warm water (approximately)
1/4 cup olive oil
3 tablespoons tamarind pulp (see page 18)
2 teaspoons ground cumin
1 teaspoon chili powder
Six 6-ounce beef filet mignons
1 tablespoon ghee (see page 15)
6 small sprigs fresh basil

This is a truly beautiful dish! The golden squash consommé, crisp orange carrots, and spiced beef all come together to create a most appealing plate. I use the tamarind to add an acidic note to the rich beef. If you would like to cut calories, eliminate the olive oil and just make a dry spice rub for the meat.

1. Preheat the oven to 400°F.
2. Using the end of a sharp knife, make small incisions on opposite sides of the squash. Place the squash on a baking sheet and bake for about 45 minutes, or until the squash is very soft. Remove from the oven and allow to cool.
3. While the squash is baking, blanch the carrots. Put them in a medium saucepan filled with boiling water over high heat. Cook for about 1 minute, or until the carrots are slightly tender but still crisp. Remove from the heat and drain well. Place the carrots in a bowl of ice water and stir to allow the carrots to cool quickly. Drain well again. Pat dry and set aside.
4. Cut the cooled squash in half and carefully remove and discard the seeds. Scoop out the pulp, and place in a blender. Add the pepper, curry powder, allspice, and salt and begin processing. Add just enough of the water to achieve the consistency of consommé. Pour the consommé in a medium saucepan over very low heat and keep warm.
5. In a small bowl, combine the olive oil with the tamarind pulp, cumin, and chili powder. Generously coat the filets with the seasoned olive oil mixture.

6. Place a nonstick skillet over medium-high heat. When very hot, but not smoking, add the filets and sear, turning frequently, for about 10 minutes, or until all sides are nicely browned and the beef remains rare in the center. Remove the pan from the heat and allow the meat to rest for a couple of minutes to seal in the juices.

7. While the beef is resting, heat the ghee in a medium sauté pan over medium heat. Add the reserved carrot julienne and sauté for 1 minute, or until just heated through.

8. Pour equal portions of the consommé in each of 6 shallow soup bowls. Place a filet in the center of each bowl. Place a mound of carrot julienne on top of each filet. Garnish with a sprig of basil and serve.

Note: The consommé can be made a day or two ahead and reheated just before serving.

Wine Suggestions: Guigal Côtes du Rhône
Atlas Peak Sangiovese
The abundant spiciness of either of these wines more than matches the complex spiciness of this beef dish.

Buffalo Rib-Eye with Black Pepper and Coriander Crust with Cranberry Coulis

Serves 6

3 tablespoons black peppercorns

4 tablespoons toasted ground coriander

Coarse salt, to taste

6 tablespoons olive oil

Six 8- to 10-ounce buffalo rib-eye steaks

3 medium beets

3 medium potatoes

3 medium parsnips

$^1/_2$ cup plus 2 tablespoons peanut oil

1 tablespoon coarsely ground *urad dal*

1 teaspoon well-toasted fenugreek seeds, finely ground

1 teaspoon coarsely ground mustard seeds

1 teaspoon crushed cumin seeds

$^1/_4$ teaspoon ground turmeric

$^1/_4$ teaspoon ground asafetida

1 ancho chile

2 cups cranberries, well washed and dried

2 cups vegetable oil

4 teaspoons ghee (see page 15)

6 sprigs fresh rosemary

In this recipe I've combined the classic American cranberry and traditional French turned vegetables to soothe the palate with each bite of the pepper-spiked, succulent but lean American buffalo. The crisp little potato bits add a nice crunch.

1. Put the black peppercorns in a small sauté pan over medium heat. Cook, stirring frequently, for about 3 minutes, or until the pepper is nicely toasted and aromatic. Place in a spice grinder and process to a smooth powder.

2. Combine the pepper powder with the coriander and salt in a small mixing bowl. Stir to blend. Add the olive oil and stir until well incorporated.

3. Generously rub the spice mixture over each steak. Place them on a nonreactive platter and cover lightly with plastic film. Allow to marinate for about 1 hour.

4. Meanwhile, peel the beets, potatoes, and parsnips and cut each vegetable into 4 pieces of equal size. Using a small sharp knife, trim off all of the uneven edges on each piece, turning the vegetable as you cut, until you have 12 neat, oval-shaped pieces of each vegetable.

5. Bring a pot of salted water to a rapid boil and, one vegetable at a time, boil the pieces for about 2 minutes, or until very lightly blanched. Lift the vegetables from the water with a slotted spoon. Drain well and pat dry. Set aside.

6. Heat $^1/_4$ cup of the peanut oil in a medium saucepan over medium-high heat. Stir in the *urad dal*, fenugreek, mustard seeds,

cumin, turmeric, asafetida, and the ancho chile. Cook, stirring frequently, for about 3 minutes, or until the spices begin to brown. Add the cranberries and salt to taste. Lower the heat and simmer for 10 minutes, or until the cranberries are soft. Pour into a blender and process to a puree. Pour into the top half of a double boiler over very hot water. Cover loosely and keep warm.

7. Preheat the oven to 200°F.

8. Line half of a baking sheet with paper towels. Set aside.

9. Heat the vegetable oil in a deep-fat fryer. When the oil has reached 360°F, add the potatoes and fry for about 4 minutes, or until they are crisp, golden, and cooked through. Using a slotted spoon, transfer the potatoes to paper towels to drain.

10. Next place the fried potatoes on the paper towel lined–side of the prepared baking sheet. Place the baking sheet in the oven.

11. Heat 2 teaspoons of the ghee in a small sauté pan over medium heat. Add the beets and sauté for about 4 minutes, or until lightly browned. Season with salt. Using a slotted spoon, transfer the beets to the unlined side of the baking sheet in the oven.

12. Wipe the sauté pan clean and return it to medium heat. Add the remaining ghee. When it is hot, add the parsnips and sauté for about 4 minutes, or until they are lightly browned. Season with salt. Using a slotted spoon, tranfer the parsnips from the sauté pan to the unlined side of the baking sheet in the oven. Make sure that the parsnips are separate from the beets, so that they don't absorb any red color.

13. Place two large nonstick sauté pans over high heat. Divide the remaining ¼ cup of peanut oil between the two pans. When the oil is very hot but not smoking, add the steaks. Sear, turning once, for about 10 minutes, or until the outsides are brown and the meat is still rare in the center.

14. Place a steak in the center of each of 6 dinner plates and arrange an equal number of turned vegetables around each tenderloin. Drizzle the cranberry coulis around the vegetables. Garnish the meat with a sprig of rosemary and serve.

Note: Early in the day, the vegetables can be blanched, the cranberry coulis made, and the potatoes fried. When ready to serve, the vegetables and potatoes can be reheated on the baking sheet as directed in the recipe, and the coulis can be warmed in the double boiler.

Wine Suggestions: Los Vascos Cabernet Sauvignon
Château Larose Trintadon

Cassoulet of Veal
with Tempered Lentils and Provençal Herbs

Serves 6

2 cups French lentils (lentilles du Puy)

1/2 cup plus 2 tablespoons olive oil

2 pounds very lean veal stew meat, cubed

2 teaspoons minced garlic, blanched

10 sprigs fresh thyme

4 tablespoons herbes de Provence

2 teaspoons Curry Spice Blend or curry powder (see page 14)

1 teaspoon toasted mustard seeds

Coarse salt, to taste

Always longing for a trip to France, I wanted to bring a scent of it to the restaurant. The classic long-cooked cassoulet, from the Languedoc region in the southwest, is rich with fatty meats and nutritiously laden with beans and herbs. In my version, I've lightened up the meat, replaced the beans with fragrant French lentils, and simplified the cooking while enriching the taste with a hint of curry and mustard.

1. Put the lentils in a medium bowl with cold water to cover by 1 inch and soak for at least 4 hours. Put the soaked lentils in a medium saucepan over medium heat with cold water to cover. Bring to a boil. Lower the heat and simmer for about 30 minutes, or until the lentils are very soft. Drain well and set aside.

2. Preheat the oven to 350°F.

3. Heat 1/4 cup of the oil in a large saucepan over medium heat. Add the veal, garlic, and thyme and sauté for about 6 minutes, or until the veal is nicely browned. Stir in the reserved lentils, 2 tablespoons of the *herbes de Provence*, curry powder, mustard seeds, and salt. Place the mixture in a 2-quart casserole. Sprinkle the remaining *herbes de Provence* over the top. Cover and bake for 15 minutes.

4. Remove from the oven. Uncover and drizzle with a bit of the remaining olive oil. Serve piping hot with sourdough bread.

Wine Suggestions: J. Vidal-Fleury Côtes du Ventoux
Domaine Tempier Bandol

Veal Medallions Wrapped in Lotus Leaf

Serves 6

3 medium carrots

3 medium potatoes

3 medium parsnips

2 cups veal stock (or 1 cup each canned defatted chicken and beef broth)

½ cup red wine

¼ teaspoon ground allspice

Pinch of freshly ground black pepper, plus more to taste

4 tablespoons (1/2 stick) butter, softened

Coarse salt, to taste

1 tablespoon ghee (see page 15)

2 teaspoons peanut oil

Six 4-ounce veal medallions

6 fresh lotus leaves, blanched (see Note)

In Hindu cultures, meals are often served in a lotus or banana leaf, which imparts a lovely fragrance to the dish it holds. In this recipe I've gone back to a rather classic rich French-style sauce and turned vegetables, which are even more traditional, to highlight the succulent veal wrapped in an exotically flavorful lotus leaf. If you can't find lotus or banana leaves, use any fragrant edible green leaf, such as collard or kale.

This is another great meal with which to impress guests. Although it appears to be complicated, the sauce and vegetables can be cooked early in the day to ease last-minute preparation.

1. Peel the carrots, potatoes, and parsnips and cut each vegetable into 4 pieces of equal size. Using a small sharp knife, trim off all of the uneven edges on each piece, turning the vegetable as you cut, until you have 12 neat oval-shaped pieces about 2 inches long of each vegetable.

2. Bring a pot of salted water to a rapid boil and, one vegetable at a time, boil the carrots, potatoes, and parsnips for about 2 minutes, or until they are very lightly blanched. Lift the vegetables from the water with a slotted spoon. Drain well and pat dry. Set aside.

3. Pour the veal stock in a medium saucepan over medium heat and bring to a boil. Lower the heat and simmer for about 15 minutes, or until the stock is reduced by one half. Add the red wine, allspice, and pinch of pepper. Bring to a boil again and then lower the heat and simmer for 5 minutes. Add the butter

and whisk to incorporate. Season with salt. Pour into the top half of a double boiler set over very hot water. Cover loosely and keep warm.

4. Preheat the oven to 200°F.

5. Heat the ghee in a large nonstick sauté pan over medium heat. Add the reserved vegetables and sauté for about 5 minutes, or until lightly browned. Season with salt and pepper. Using a slotted spoon, transfer the vegetables to a low-sided baking sheet and place in the oven.

6. Heat the oil in a large nonstick sauté pan over medium-high heat. Season the veal medallions with salt and pepper and place them in the pan. Sear, turning once, for about 5 minutes per side, or until the centers are medium-rare. Remove from the pan and, working quickly and carefully, securely wrap each medallion in a lotus leaf, trimming off the excess leaf to make a neat, tight packet.

7. Spoon a pool of the warm sauce into the center of each of 6 dinner plates. Place a lotus-wrapped medallion in the center of the sauce. Arrange an equal number of turned vegetables around each packet and serve.

Note: Lotus leaves are available in Asian markets or through one of the sources listed on page 209. If you have difficulty locating them or you decide to make this dish at the last minute, use turnip or collard greens as a substitute.

Wine Suggestions: Faiveley Mercurey
Steele Pinot Noir
The silky seduction of the Pinot Noir varietal will enhance this wonderfully complex yet simple veal dish.

Roasted Leg of Lamb with Mint Chutney and Mint-Flavored Potatoes

Serves 6

1 cup fresh mint leaves, plus ¼ cup
   julienned leaves
4 tablespoons peanut oil
2 tablespoons urad dal
1 tablespoon coriander seeds
1 tablespoon mustard seeds
1 teaspoon cumin seeds
3 fresh cayenne chiles
½ cup tamarind pulp (see page 18)
¼ cup jaggery (see page 18)
Coarse salt, to taste
1 cup water
One 5½- to 6-pound leg of spring
   lamb
6 medium potatoes, peeled and cut
   into ½-inch dice
¼ cup ghee (see page 15)
Freshly ground black pepper, to taste
1 cup dry white wine
8 tablespoons (1 stick) butter,
   softened

This dish includes my grandmother's mint chutney recipe. Her Brahmin soul is probably most uncomfortable knowing that I've used it to rub a leg of lamb! The fragrant mint seems a perfect foil for the tender, almost sweet spring lamb. The intensely spiced chutney adds real character to what could easily be called a simple dish of meat and potatoes. I make this instead of the traditional American Thanksgiving turkey—the aromas coming from the kitchen are just as tantalizing.

1. Wash the mint and pick off all the leaves. Pat them dry and set aside.

2. Heat 2 tablespoons of the oil in a medium sauté pan over medium heat. Add the *urad dal* and coriander seeds and sauté for about 4 minutes, or until the dal and coriander are slightly browned and aromatic. Stir in the mustard and cumin seeds and cayenne peppers and continue to sauté for an additional 3 minutes. Scrape the spice mixture into a blender and process to puree.

3. Return the sauté pan to medium heat and add 1 tablespoon of the remaining oil. Stir in the mint leaves and sauté for 2 minutes. Scrape the mint into the blender. Add the tamarind, jaggery, and salt and process to blend. Add the water and process for about 5 minutes, or until the mixture is very smooth. Scoop out 2 tablespoons of the mint chutney and set it aside.

4. Preheat the oven to 400°F.

5. Brush the lamb with the remaining 1 tablespoon of oil. Generously rub the remaining mint chutney over the lamb. Place on a rack in a roasting pan and roast in the oven for about 1 hour, or until an instant-read thermometer inserted into the center reaches 125°F for rare (or 135°F for medium). Remove from the oven and let rest for at least 5 minutes before carving.

6. While the lamb is roasting, prepare the potatoes. Put them in cold, salted water to cover over medium-high heat. Bring to a boil. Lower the heat and simmer for about 5 minutes, or just until the potatoes are tender. Drain well and pat dry. Toss with the reserved 2 tablespoons of mint chutney.

7. Heat the ghee in a medium sauté pan over medium-high heat. Add the potatoes and salt and pepper to taste. Cook, stirring frequently, for about 6 minutes, or until the potatoes are slightly crisp and golden brown. Remove from the heat. Cover lightly to keep warm.

8. Place the lamb on a carving board.

9. Pour the pan juices into a medium saucepan over medium heat. Carefully spoon off any excess fat at the top. Add the wine and bring to a boil. Boil for 1 minute. Whisk in the butter and salt and pepper to taste. Lower heat and simmer for 3 minutes, whisking frequently so that the sauce does not separate.

10. Using a sharp chef's knife, carve off 3 pieces of lamb for each serving, and place them in the centers of 6 dinner plates. Surround each serving of lamb with an equal portion of the potatoes. Drizzle the pan sauce over the top and garnish with julienned mint. Serve immediately.

Wine Suggestions: Saintsbury Pinot Noir
Meridian Pinot Noir
The cherry fruitiness of the Pinot Noir grape will match perfectly with this mint-flavored lamb course.

Baby Lamb Racks
with Curry Leaf–Black Pepper Crust
and Curried Blackberry Sauce

Serves 6

2 tablespoons peanut oil

1 cup blackberries, well washed, picked clean of stems, and patted dry

1 teaspoon Curry Spice Blend (see page 14) or curry powder

1/4 cup water

Coarse salt, to taste

3 tablespoons black peppercorns

1/4 cup minced fresh curry leaves

1/4 cup olive oil

Three 8-rib baby lamb racks, frenched (meat removed from tops of bones)

3 cups canola oil

Twenty-four (approximately 6 potatoes) 1/4-inch-thick slices purple Peruvian potatoes

Freshly ground black pepper, to taste

6 sprigs fresh purple basil

1 pound asparagus, trimmed and blanched, optional

I first made this dish a few years ago in Charlie Trotter's kitchen for a group of invited guests. It was such a hit that I took it back to Memphis, where it frequently appears on my menu. The purple potatoes don't retain their deep purple color when cooked, but they become an interesting grayish blue, which is heightened by their crisp golden edges, when they are fried. The blackberry sauce and the purple basil combine to make this an intensely rich plate. If you can't find purple potatoes, use yellow Finns or Yukon Golds instead.

1. Heat the peanut oil in a medium saucepan over medium heat. Add the blackberries and curry powder and stir to combine. Add the water and bring to a boil. Lower the heat and simmer for 3 minutes. Pour the sauce into a blender and process until smooth. Season with salt. Pour into a nonreactive container and set aside, letting it cool to room temperature.

2. Preheat the oven to 400°F.

3. Place the peppercorns in a small sauté pan over medium heat. Cook, stirring frequently, for about 3 minutes, or until the peppercorns are nicely toasted. Process in a spice grinder until finely ground. Combine the ground pepper with the curry leaves and salt to taste in a small bowl. Add the olive oil and stir to blend.

4. Rub the spice mixture on the lamb racks. Wrap the bones with aluminum foil to keep them from burning while roasting.

5. Place the lamb racks in a roasting pan and roast in the oven

for about 30 minutes, or until an instant-read thermometer inserted into the center reaches 125°F for rare (or 135°. for medium). Remove from the oven and let rest for 5 minutes before carving.

6. While the lamb is roasting, prepare the potatoes. Line 2 baking sheets with a double layer of paper towels. Place the oil in a deep-fat fryer over high heat. When the oil registers 365°F on a candy thermometer, add the potatoes, a few slices at a time, taking care not to crowd the pan. Fry, turning if necessary, for about 4 minutes, or until tender and beginning to brown. Using a slotted spoon, transfer the potatoes to one of the prepared baking sheets. Continue frying until all of the potatoes have been browned and are well drained (on the same baking sheet). A few at a time, return the potatoes to the hot oil and fry, turning if necessary, for about 2 more minutes, or until crisp. Drain the potatoes on the clean paper towel–lined baking sheet. Season with salt and pepper.

7. Spoon equal portions of the blackberry sauce in the center of each of 6 dinner plates. Carve the lamb racks into chops, allowing 4 per person. Stack 4 potato slices in the center of each plate and crisscross the lamb chops over the potato stacks. Garnish each plate with a sprig of purple basil and a small bunch of blanched asparagus, if desired, and serve.

Note: Fresh blackberries may be replaced with high-quality frozen backberries.

Wine Suggestions: Stag's Leap Wine Cellars Napa Cabernet Sauvignon
Justin Winery and Vineyard Isosceles
A full-bodied Cabernet-based wine is a must for the sweet and spicy combination served with the slightly fatty lamb.

Lamb Stew with Vindaloo Spices and Sweet Squash and Turnips

Serves 6

2 tablespoons *urad dal*
(see Note, page 27)

2 tablespoons ground chiles

1 tablespoon ground coriander

1 tablespoon mustard seeds

1/2 tablespoon cumin seeds

1 teaspoon ground tamarind

1/2 teaspoon ground fenugreek

1/2 teaspoon ground asafetida

1 teaspoon jaggery (see page 18)

1/4 cup sesame oil

2 tablespoons water

3 pounds very lean lamb stew meat,
cut into 2-inch cubes

6 tablespoons peanut oil

Coarse salt, to taste

1 1/2 cups 1/2-inch dice winter squash

1 1/2 cups 1/2-inch dice turnips

1 tablespoon olive oil

1 tablespoon light brown sugar

1/4 teaspoon ground nutmeg

1 cup veal stock (or 1/2 cup each
canned defatted chicken and beef
broth)

1 tablespoon finely chopped cilantro

The principles of fusion cooking do not really lend themselves to a vindaloo style, but I got so many requests for this fiery dish that I decided to take the challenge. I cook the lamb in this vindaloo to a medium consistency, rather than to the traditional, falling-apart stage. I rid the dish of its grease by reducing the oil and incorporating veal stock. I also toast and grind each spice separately to make the most out of their individual flavors. It's all very time consuming, but I think you will find the finished dish well worth the effort.

1. Using a small sauté pan over medium heat, toast, one at a time, the *urad dal*, ground chiles, coriander, mustard, cumin, tamarind, fenugreek, and asafetida until lightly browned and very aromatic. Keep them separate. Then, using a spice grinder, process each spice individually to a very fine powder. Combine all of the spices with the jaggery in a small bowl. Drizzle in the sesame oil and water and, using a fork, stir the mixture into a dry crumble.

2. Put the lamb in a mixing bowl. Sprinkle the spice mixture over the lamb and, using your hands, rub the mixture into the meat. Set aside to marinate at room temperature for about 30 minutes.

3. Heat the peanut oil in a large, heavy saucepan over medium heat. Add the seasoned lamb and cook, stirring frequently, for about 7 minutes, or until the lamb begins to brown. Season with salt. Lower the heat and cook for 30 minutes, adding a bit

of water if the pan gets too dry.
4. While the lamb is cooking, prepare the squash and turnips. Place the squash and turnips in a medium saucepan in rapidly boiling salted water for 2 minutes. Drain well and pat dry.
4. Heat the olive oil in a medium sauté pan over medium heat. Add the blanched vegetables, brown sugar, nutmeg, and salt to taste. Lower the heat and sauté for about 10 minutes, or until the squash and turnips are very tender and slightly colored.
5. After the lamb has cooked for 30 minutes, add the veal stock. Raise the heat and bring to a boil. Cover and lower the heat. Cook for 5 minutes.
6. Spoon equal portions of the lamb into each of 6 shallow soup bowls. Place equal portions of the vegetable mixture over each portion of lamb. Sprinkle the cilantro over the top and serve.

Wine Suggestions: Ravenswood Vintners' Blend Zinfandel
Cline Cellars Zinfandel
The intensity of the vindaloo meets its match with the zesty spice of either of these Zinfandels.

Poultry

Parcels of Chicken with Garlic and Amaranth

Oven-Roasted Chicken with Lime-Scented
Spring Vegetables

Supreme of Chicken with Sweet Spices

Cornish Game Hens with Spicy Lentil Ragout

Chicken with Coconut Milk, Lemongrass, and
Ginger

Poussins Smoked on Sandalwood Chips with
Israeli Couscous

Parcels of Chicken
with Garlic and Amaranth

Serves 6

4 tablespoons peanut oil

$^1/_4$ cup finely chopped onion

2 teaspoons minced garlic

2 tablespoons chopped fresh cilantro

1 teaspoon ajowan

1 teaspoon ground coriander

1 teaspoon turmeric

Six 6-ounce boneless, skinless
chicken breast halves

$^1/_4$ cup dry white wine

Coarse salt and freshly ground black
pepper, to taste

3 cups fresh amaranth leaves

2 packages frozen puff-pastry dough,
thawed

1 bunch fresh chives, lightly blanched

Cumin-Scented Tomato Coulis (see
page 34)

The amaranth leaves in this dish take me back to our Hyderabad kitchen garden, filled with tropical fragrances and ripening fruit. I loved to roam the garden in the afternoon, but if caught by my grandmother, she would call me inside, as she felt that the sun would make my skin too dark, and consequently, make me unmarriageable.

If you can't find fresh amaranth leaves, use any fresh greens available, such as spinach or kale. You could also enclose these packets with phyllo or strudel dough, homemade or commercial pie dough, or even blanched large cabbage or romaine leaves, for a low-calorie treat. Smaller versions of these packets would make terrific cocktail tidbits.

1. Preheat the oven to 400°F.

2. Heat 3 tablespoons of the peanut oil in a large oven-proof sauté pan over medium heat. Add the onion, garlic, cilantro, *ajowan*, coriander, and turmeric and sauté for about 3 minutes, or until the vegetables begin to soften. Add the chicken, wine, and salt and pepper and continue to sauté for about 6 minutes, or until the chicken is nicely browned.

3. Bake for about 10 minutes, or until the chicken is cooked through. Remove from the oven and allow to cool, but do not turn off the oven.

4. Line a baking sheet with parchment paper.

5. Heat the remaining oil in a large sauté pan over medium

heat. Add the amaranth leaves and sauté for about 5 minutes, or until tender. Remove from the heat and set aside.

6. When the chicken is cool enough to handle, slice it on the bias into thin strips. Return the strips to the pan and stir to coat them well with the onion mixture. Set aside.

7. Using a rolling pin, roll out the puff-pastry dough into a thin flat sheet and cut each sheet into 3 pieces. Place an equal portion of the chicken mixture and amaranth leaves in the center of each pastry sheet. Fold over the two long sides to cover the chicken mixture. Fold over the shorter sides to make a neat package. Turn it over so the folded edges are on the bottom. Using two chive pieces, tie a "ribbon" around the parcel, making a bow in the center of the top of each packet.

8. Place the packets on the prepared baking sheet and bake for 10 minutes. Remove from the oven, and using a sharp serrated knife, cut each packet in half, on the bias. Place 2 halves in the center of each of 6 dinner plates, slightly overlapping the cut edges. Drizzle tomato coulis around the edge of the plate and serve.

Wine Suggestions: Domaine Leflaive Puligny-Montrachet
Sonoma-Cutrer Les Pierres Chardonnay
Either of these elegant, floral-flavored wines will offer the richness needed to bring this chicken dish to its full brilliance.

Oven-Roasted Chicken with Lime-Scented Spring Vegetables

Serves 6

10 very thin asparagus stalks, well washed

3 carrots, trimmed and peeled

1 bunch scallions, trimmed

¼ teaspoon ground turmeric

Six 8- to 10-ounce chicken breast halves, skin on and bone in

2 tablespoons plus 2 teaspoons olive oil

6 cloves garlic, skin on and slightly smashed

6 sprigs fresh rosemary

6 sprigs fresh thyme

6 tablespoons extra virgin olive oil

½ pound fresh sugar-snap peas, well washed

Coarse salt, to taste

Freshly ground black pepper

6 tablespoons fresh lime juice

As simple as it gets, this aromatic dish makes a great family meal. Use any vegetables, just make sure that they are young and tender as you want their sweetness to offset the lime.

1. Preheat the oven to 375°F.

2. Cut the asparagus, carrots, and scallions on the bias into pieces about 1 ½ inches long. Set aside.

3. Sprinkle turmeric on the chicken breasts and rub it in, using the 2 teaspoons of olive oil as a lubricant.

4. Using your fingertips, carefully lift the skin away from each breast without totally dislodging it. Place a garlic clove and a sprig each of rosemary and thyme under the skin.

5. Place the breasts in a shallow roasting pan. Season with salt. Add the extra virgin olive oil to the pan and roast the chicken for about 20 minutes, or until an instant-read thermometer inserted into the thickest part reaches 165°F.

6. While the chicken is roasting, prepare the vegetables.

7. Heat the remaining olive oil in a large sauté pan over medium heat. Add the sugar-snap peas and the reserved vegetables. Season with salt and pepper and sauté for 5 minutes, or until the vegetables are crisp-tender. Toss in the lime juice.

8. Make a mound of vegetables in the center of a serving platter. Place the chicken breasts around the vegetables and serve with a tossed green salad and warm bread.

Wine Suggestions: Château Brane-Cantenac
Buena Vista Cabernet Sauvignon

Supreme of Chicken with Sweet Spices

Serves 6

2 tablespoons coriander seeds

1 tablespoon black cumin seeds

1 tablespoon black peppercorns

1 teaspoon whole cloves

One 3-inch cinnamon stick

6 tablespoons canola oil

2 tablespoons minced onion

1 tablespoon minced garlic

1 tablespoon minced fresh ginger

1 tablespoon minced serrano chile

1/2 cup plain nonfat yogurt

3 tablespoons fresh lime juice

Coarse salt, to taste

Six 6-ounce boneless, skinless
   chicken breast halves

1 cup chopped leeks, white and pale
   green parts only

1 cup heavy cream

4 tablespoons (1/2 stick) butter,
   softened

Freshly ground black pepper, to taste

2 cups tiny fresh cauliflower florets

1 cup tiny fresh peas

6 sprigs fresh thyme

Although this recipe has a long list of ingredients, it is really very simple to make. I like it for Sunday meals at home. However, if you don't have time to create the whole dish, the marinated chicken would be wonderful right off the grill, served with a crisp salad and crusty bread.

1. Combine the coriander, black cumin, peppercorns, cloves, and cinnamon in a small nonstick sauté pan over medium heat. Cook, stirring frequently, for about 4 minutes, or until the spices are nicely toasted and aromatic. Remove from the heat and allow to cool.

2. Put the spices in a spice grinder and process until very fine. Set aside.

3. Heat 2 tablespoons of the oil in a large sauté pan over medium heat. Add the onions, garlic, ginger, and chile. Sauté for about 5 minutes, or until the vegetables are golden. Add the spice powder and stir to blend. Remove from the heat and allow the mixture to cool.

4. Stir the yogurt, lime juice, and salt into the spice mixture. Place the chicken in a glass baking dish and pour the yogurt mixture over the top. Cover with plastic film and refrigerate for about 1 hour.

5. Put the leeks in a small saucepan filled with rapidly boiling salted water, and blanch for 30 seconds. Drain well and pat dry.

6. Combine the leeks with the heavy cream in a medium saucepan over medium heat. Cook for about 3 minutes, or just

until the cream begins to boil. (Watch carefully because the cream can rapidly boil over. Quickly lift the pan from the heat if this happens.) Immediately whisk in the butter and salt and pepper to taste. Lower the heat and gently simmer for about 4 minutes, or until the sauce coats the back of a spoon. Pour into the top half of a double boiler over very hot water. Cover lightly and keep warm.

7. Preheat the oven to 450°F.

8. Remove the chicken from the refrigerator, and scrape off marinade.

9. Heat 2 tablespoons of the remaining oil in a large ovenproof sauté pan over medium heat. Add the chicken breasts to the hot pan and sauté for about 5 minutes, or until the chicken begins to brown. Place the pan in the oven and roast the chicken for about 10 minutes, or until it is cooked through and golden brown.

10. While the chicken is cooking, prepare the vegetables. Heat the remaining oil in a medium sauté pan over medium heat. Add the cauliflower and sauté for 2 minutes. Add the peas and sauté for an additional 5 minutes, or until the vegetables are still crisp-tender. Season with salt and pepper.

11. Place equal portions of the cauliflower-pea mixture in the center of each of 6 dinner plates. Nestle a chicken breast into the center of the vegetables on each plate. Drizzle the warm leek sauce over the top of the chicken and around the edge of the plate. Insert a sprig of thyme into the chicken and serve.

Wine Suggestions: Louis Jadot Beaune Boucherottes
Morgan Pinot Noir
The velvety texture of the Pinot Noir makes a perfect companion to this sweetly spiced chicken dish.

Cornish Game Hens
with Spicy Lentil Ragout

Serves 6

2 cups *toor dal*, well rinsed (see Note)

2 quarts plus ¼ cup cold water

¾ cup plus 3 tablespoons canola oil

1 cup finely chopped onions

1 tablespoon fresh thyme leaves

3 tablespoons cayenne pepper flakes

2 tablespoons crushed cumin seeds

1 tablespoon ground coriander

Coarse salt, to taste

Six 10- to 12-ounce Cornish game
   hens, well rinsed and dried

1 cup ½-inch dice onions

2 tablespoons Curry Spice Blend (see
   page 14) or curry powder

1 tablespoon freshly ground black
   pepper

1 teaspoon mustard seeds

3 cups cooked basmati rice

2 cups peeled, seeded, and finely
   chopped plum tomatoes

2 cups cooked sliced zucchini
   (optional)

To me, there is nothing more reminiscent of the French countryside than a beautifully roasted hen or chicken. In this recipe, I have taken the simplicity of the French home kitchen and given it a hint of home-style Indian cooking. The lentil ragout is based on a very basic soup that I watched my father's workers make daily across the street from our house. This is another recipe that can be partially assembled ahead of time, for ease of last-minute preparation. It often ends up on my menu on a very busy Saturday night, where I need a piping hot, flavorful, precise dish that I can manage to get out with breakneck speed.

1. Put the *toor dal* and 2 quarts of cold water in a medium saucepan over medium heat. Cook, stirring occasionally, for about 30 minutes, or until the mixture has become a puree. Remove from the heat and set aside.

2. Preheat the oven to 400°F.

3. Heat ¼ cup of the canola oil in a medium saucepan over medium heat. Add the finely chopped onion, thyme, pepper flakes, cumin seeds, coriander, and salt. Sauté for about 5 minutes, or until the mixture has formed a paste. Put the mixture in a blender with the remaining ¼ cup of water and process to make a smooth paste.

4. Rub each game hen with a generous coating of the spice paste. Using a pastry brush and about 2 tablespoons of the remaining oil, lightly coat the seasoned birds. Place them on a rack on a low-sided baking sheet and roast in the oven for

about 45 minutes, or until the skin is crispy and an instant-read thermometer inserted into the meatiest part reaches 165°F.

5. While the birds are roasting, prepare the lentil ragout and rice.

6. Heat 6 tablespoons of the canola oil in a large saucepan over medium heat. Add the onion, curry powder, and pepper and sauté for 6 minutes, or until the onion is golden brown. Add the reserved *toor dal* puree and salt to taste. Lower the heat and cook, stirring frequently, for 30 minutes.

7. Heat the remaining 3 tablespoons of canola oil in a large sauté pan over medium heat. Add the mustard seeds and sauté for 3 minutes. Stir in the rice, tomatoes, and salt to taste. Cook, stirring frequently, for 10 minutes.

8. Spoon equal portions of the lentil ragout in each of 6 large, shallow soup bowls. Spoon equal portions of the rice mixture into the center of the ragout and lay a Cornish hen on top of the rice in each bowl. If using, nestle the zucchini slices into the hen and serve immediately.

Note: Toor dal is available at Indian, Pakistani, or Middle Eastern markets, some specialty food stores, or through one of the mail order sources listed on page 209.

The lentil ragout can be made up to 2 days in advance and reheated. The rice can be put together early in the day and reheated in the oven for about 10 minutes before serving.

Wine Suggestions: Penfolds Shiraz
Les Jamelles Syrah
The pepper and spiciness of the Shiraz and Syrah varietals in these wines will enhance the dominant of flavors in this dish.

Chicken with Coconut Milk, Lemongrass, and Ginger

Serves 6

¹/₄ cup peanut oil

¹/₄ cup finely chopped onions

4 dried cayenne chiles

2 tablespoons minced fresh ginger

2 tablespoons minced fresh lemongrass

2 cups diced peeled cooked potatoes

1 tablespoon toasted black cumin seeds, ground

¹/₄ teaspoon ground turmeric

6 ounces coconut milk (see page 18)

6 ounces half-and-half

Coarse salt, to taste

Two 2 ¹/₂-pound whole chickens, cut into serving pieces

This is a trip down memory lane for me as the aromas coming from the oven take me straight back to Mrs. Ayyer's kitchen. It is an easy-to-make family-style dish. Any left over will make a marvelous salad. Use the stewing liquid as a dressing.

1. Heat the oil in a large sauté pan over medium heat. Add the onions and chiles and lower the heat. Cook, stirring frequently, for about 10 minutes, or until the onions are golden brown and well caramelized.

2. Stir in the ginger and lemongrass and sauté for 2 minutes. Add the potatoes and stir to combine. Stir in the black cumin and turmeric. When the spices are well incorporated, stir in the coconut milk and the half-and-half. Add salt and remove from the heat.

3. Preheat the oven to 300°F.

4. Place the chicken in a Dutch oven or another large heavy ovenproof casserole. Pour the coconut mixture over the top of the chicken. Cover and bake for about 1 hour, or until the chicken is very tender.

5. Serve, family style, with basmati rice, a green salad, and warm Indian breads.

Note: In India, the chiles would be left in the finished dish, but if you are concerned about them being eaten, remove them before serving.

Wine Suggestions: Qupé Syrah
Louis M. Martini Red Zinfandel

Poussins Smoked on Sandalwood Chips with Israeli Couscous

7 cups water

6 tablespoons fresh ginger juice (See page 12)

2 teaspoons saffron threads

1 teaspoon rosewater

$1/4$ teaspoon ground cardamom

Coarse salt, to taste

Six 10- to 12-ounce poussins

$1/4$ cup ghee (see page 15)

Pinch of ground turmeric

$1 1/2$ cups Israeli couscous

3 tablespoons olive oil

1 tablespoon minced onion

$1/2$ teaspoon minced garlic, blanched

$1/4$ teaspoon ajowan

$1/4$ cup peeled, seeded, and finely diced plum tomatoes

1 tablespoon minced fresh flat-leaf parsley

If you don't have *poussins* (very young, very small chickens) readily available, you can use Cornish game hens for this recipe. Since sandalwood chips are quite expensive, you might want to conserve them by improvising a small smoker, using a small grill or hibachi tented with aluminum foil; a large smoker or grill requires lots of chips. The fragrance that sandalwood lends to the delicate chicken is indescribable, so I do recommend your trying it—at least once!

Israeli couscous is very large-grained and has a much different flavor and texture from the finely ground semolina you might be used to. If there is any delay between cooking and serving, you may have to add a bit of liquid because it absorbs moisture quickly.

1. Combine 4 cups of the water with the ginger juice, saffron, rosewater, cardamom, and salt in a medium saucepan over medium heat. Bring to a boil. Remove from the heat immediately and allow to cool to 120°F, so the *poussins* will not cook as they soak.

2. Put the *poussins* in a dish large enough to hold them snugly, in one layer. Pour the seasoned water over the *poussins* and place in the refrigerator, allowing them to soak, turning occasionally, for 4 hours.

3. Remove the *poussins* from the soak and pat them dry.

4. Heat the ghee in a small saucepan. Stir in the turmeric. When well combined, using a pastry brush, lightly coat each *poussin*

with the seasoned ghee.

5. Prepare the smoker according to manufacturer's directions, using the sandalwood chips for flavoring.

6. When the smoker is hot, place the *poussins* on the rack and smoke, following the manufacturer's directions, for about 1 ½ hours, or until an instant-read thermometer inserted into the thickest part of the bird reaches 165°F.

7. While the *poussins* are smoking, prepare the couscous.

8. Pour the remaining 3 cups of water in a medium saucepan over medium-high heat. Bring to a boil. Add the couscous and salt to taste and bring to a boil. Lower the heat and cover. Simmer for about 12 minutes, or

until the couscous is tender and the water has been absorbed. Remove from the heat.

9. Heat the oil in a large sauté pan over medium heat. Add the onion, garlic, and *ajowan* and sauté for 3 minutes. Stir in the couscous and tomato and cook, stirring frequently, for about 10 minutes, or until the flavors are well combined. Remove from the heat and stir in the parsley. Taste and adjust the seasoning with salt, if necessary.

10. Place equal portions of the couscous on each of 6 dinner plates. Nestle a smoked *poussin* into the couscous and serve.

Wine Suggestions: Casa Lapostolle Merlot
Pahlmeyer Merlot
The soft and spicy combination of the Merlot grape marries extremely well with this aromatic dish.

Game

Tea-Smoked Quail with Hyderabad Biryani

Oven-Roasted Quail with Tandoori-Honey
Emulsion and Quinoa with Almond Sprouts
and Baby Bok Choy

Duck Breasts with Caramelized Curry Sauce and
Confit of Sweet Potatoes

Supreme of Pheasant with Basmati-Truffle
Risotto

Venison Racks with Indian Grits and Sun-Dried
Tomato Chutney

Antelope Chops with Blackberry-Ginger
Chutney

Tea-Smoked Quail
with Hyderabad Biryani

Serves 6

1 cup freshly brewed strong green tea

3 tablespoons plus 1 teaspoon jaggery (see page 18)

1 tablespoon freshly ground black pepper

2 teaspoons ground turmeric

Coarse salt, to taste

12 quail, well washed and dried

1 teaspoon ground allspice

1 teaspoon ground coriander

$1/2$ teaspoon ground cinnamon

3 tablespoons peanut oil

2 teaspoons water

2 ounces (about 1/2 cup) green tea leaves

2 cups chicken stock

$3/4$ cup dry white wine

Freshly ground white pepper to taste

4 tablespoons ($1/2$ stick) butter, softened

$1/2$ cup $1/2$-inch dice carrots

6 tablespoons ghee (see page 15)

2 tablespoons minced onion

1 teaspoon minced garlic

1 teaspoon minced fresh ginger

1 teaspoon minced serrano chile

(INGREDIENTS CONTINUE ON PAGE 126)

I have learned that there is more than one way to impart flavor. With quail, which can't take a lot of spice, I love the aromatic smoking that tea provides. The tea has a depth of flavor that adds an enticing dimension to the delicate quail. Biryani (a classic meat-enriched rice casserole) is a staple from my childhood that I use here to make a strong contrast to the classic rich butter sauce.

1. Combine the tea, 3 tablespoons of the jaggery, the pepper, 1 teaspoon of the turmeric, and the salt in a nonreactive container large enough to hold the quail securely in one layer. Add the quail. Cover loosely and place in the refrigerator, allowing to soak, turning occasionally, for 6 hours.

2. Prepare the smoker according to manufacturer's directions for smoking chicken.

3. Combine the allspice, coriander, cinnamon, remaining jaggery, and salt to taste in a small bowl. Stir in the oil and water to form a smooth paste.

4. Remove the quail from the soak and pat dry. Generously coat each quail with the spice mixture.

5. Sprinkle the loose tea over the coals in the smoker. Immediately place the seasoned quail on the rack and smoke for about 45 minutes or until an instant-read thermometer inserted into the thickest part of the bird reaches 165°F.

6. While the quail are smoking, prepare the sauce and *biryani*.

7. Place the stock, wine, and salt and pepper to taste in a small

1 tablespoon Garam Masala (see page 14)
2 cups cooked basmati rice
1/2 cup fresh peas
2 tablespoons fresh lemon juice
1 1/2 tablespoons chopped fresh chives

saucepan over medium heat. Bring to a simmer. Whisk in the butter and, when well incorporated, lower the heat. Gently simmer for 15 minutes, or until the sauce coats the back of a spoon. Pour the sauce into the top half of a double boiler set over boiling water. Cover loosely and keep warm.

8. Put the carrots in a small saucepan filled with rapidly boiling salted water and blanch for 1 minute. Drain well and refresh under cold running water. Pat dry and set aside.

9. Heat 3 tablespoons of ghee in a large sauté pan over medium heat. Add the onion, garlic, ginger, and chile and sauté for 4 minutes, or until the vegetables are quite soft. Stir in the garam masala and remaining turmeric and sauté for 1 minute. Stir in the rice, peas, reserved carrots, and remaining ghee. Drizzle the lemon juice over the top and stir to combine. Cook, stirring occasionally, for 5 minutes, or until the biryani is hot and the flavors are well incorporated.

10. Spoon equal portions of the sauce into the center of each of 6 dinner plates. Place equal portions of the *biryani* into the center of the sauce on each plate. Lay a quail on the *biryani* and sprinkle with chives. Serve immediately.

Wine Suggestions: Chalone Chardonnay
Rosemount Chardonnay
The buttery oak and richness of a top-notch Chardonnay, such as either of these wines, will highlight the mellowness of the tea-smoked quail.

Oven-Roasted Quail with Tandoori-Honey Emulsion and Quinoa with Almond Sprouts and Baby Bok Choy

Serves 6

½ cup almond sprouts (see Note)

4 cups water

Coarse salt to taste

2 cups quinoa, well washed and drained

6 tablespoons ghee (see page 16)

1 teaspoon minced fresh ginger

1 teaspoon minced fresh flat-leaf parsley

2 cups chicken stock

½ cup dry white wine

1 teaspoon fresh ginger juice (see page 13)

¼ teaspoon minced garlic

Freshly ground white pepper, to taste

8 tablespoons (1 stick) butter, softened

12 quail, well washed and dried

2 tablespoons honey

2 tablespoons tandoori masala (see Note)

1 teaspoon ground mustard

12 leaves baby bok choy, trimmed, washed, and dried

2 tablespoons peanut oil

The sweetness of the almond sprouts and the honey emulsion makes a spectacular backdrop for the quinoa and delicate quail. Although the dish is slightly complicated to pull together, I think that you will find that its intense flavors give you your reward. Lou, my fiancé, and I made this dish together in his recently well-stocked kitchen, drinking more than a glass of wine as we cooked. It's an absolutely marvelous dinner party meal.

1. Put the almond sprouts in a food processor fitted with the metal blade and process to a coarse puree. Set aside.

2. Pour the water into a medium saucepan over high heat. Add salt and bring to a boil. Add the quinoa, cover, and lower the heat. Cook for 12 minutes, or until all of the liquid has been absorbed and the quinoa is translucent. Stir in the ghee, ginger, parsley, and the reserved almond sprout puree. Place over very low heat and cook, stirring occasionally, for 5 minutes. Remove from the heat and set aside.

3. Combine the stock, wine, ginger juice, garlic, and salt and white pepper to taste in a medium saucepan over medium heat and bring to a simmer. Whisk in the butter and, when well incorporated, lower the heat and simmer for 15 minutes, or until the sauce coats the back of a spoon. Pour into the top half of a double boiler set over boiling water. Cover loosely and keep warm.

4. Preheat the oven to 400°F.

5. Stuff the cavity of each quail with the quinoa mixture.

6. Combine the honey, tandoori masala, mustard, and salt to taste in a small bowl. When well combined, generously rub each stuffed quail with the mixture. Place the quail on a rack in a large roasting pan and roast in the oven for 15 minutes, or until an instant-read thermometer inserted into the thickest part registers 165°F. Remove from the oven and let rest 5 minutes.

7. While the quail is roasting, prepare the bok choy. Heat the peanut oil in a large sauté pan over medium heat. Add the bok choy and sauté for 5 minutes, or until it is crisp-tender. Season to taste with salt and white pepper and remove from the heat.

8. Spoon an equal portion of the sauce into the center of each of 6 dinner plates. Place 2 quail in the center of the sauce. Nestle 2 bok choy against the quail on each plate and serve.

Note: Almond sprouts are available at some health food stores or through one of the Sources listed on page 209. The sprouts will add just a hint of an almond taste to any dish.
Tandoori masala is a spice mixture that is available in East Indian or Pakistani markets.

Wine Suggestions: Ridge Lytton Springs Zinfandel
Vieux Télégraphe Châteauneuf-du-Pape
Either of these highly concentrated wines will offer balance and body to this rather sweet, complex dish.

Duck Breasts with Caramelized Curry Sauce and Confit of Sweet Potatoes

Serves 6

¹/₂ cup ghee (see page 15)

¹/₂ cup diced, plus 6 tablespoons very
 finely minced, red onion

4 cups plus 5 tablespoons peanut oil

2 tablespoons ground coriander

1 teaspoon freshly ground black
 pepper

1¹/₄ teaspoons ground allspice

Six 10-ounce boneless, skinless duck
 breasts

1¹/₂ cups honey

¹/₂ cup fresh lemon juice, strained

1 cup water

¹/₂ cup dry white wine

1 teaspoon Curry Spice Blend (see
 page 14) or curry powder

Coarse salt, to taste

8 tablespoons (1 stick) butter,
 softened

4 medium raw sweet potatoes

4 medium sweet potatoes, baked

6 sprigs fresh chervil

Once the skin has been removed, duck breasts are extremely lean and relatively mild in flavor. This is an elegant dish that can be partially assembled ahead of time.

1. Heat 2 tablespoons of ghee in a small nonstick sauté pan over medium heat. Add the ¹/₂ cup diced red onion and sauté for about 10 minutes, or until well caramelized (see page 17). Remove from the heat and place in a small food processor fitted with the metal blade. Process to a smooth puree. Scrape from the bowl and measure out ¹/₄ cup. Set aside.

2. Heat 2 tablespoons of the peanut oil in a small sauté pan over medium heat. Add the 6 tablespoons finely minced red onion and sauté for about 10 minutes, or until very soft. Remove from the heat and let sit until cool enough to handle.

3. Combine the coriander, pepper, and 1 teaspoon allspice with the minced red onion. Blend well and generously rub each duck breast with the spice mixture. Place the breasts on a plate and cover lightly with plastic film. Refrigerate for at least 1 hour, but no more than 8, to allow the breasts to absorb the spices.

4. Combine the honey and lemon juice in a medium saucepan over medium heat. When well blended, whisk in the water, wine, and reserved red onion puree. Cook, stirring frequently, for about 15 minutes, or until the sauce has reduced by one half. Stir in the curry powder and salt. Whisk in the butter, a bit at a time, until well incorporated. Pour into the top of a double boiler set over very hot water. Cover and keep warm.

5. Peel the raw sweet potatoes. Trim about ½ inch off each end and, using a Japanese vegetable turner, cut each potato into long, thin, pastalike strands. Place the strands in cold water to barely cover.

6. Heat the 4 cups of peanut oil in a deep-fat fryer over high heat. When the temperature reaches 365°F on a candy thermometer, remove a handful of sweet potato strands from the soaking water and pat them until very dry. Drop the strands into the hot oil and cook for about 45 seconds, or until the potatoes begin to crisp slightly but are still pliable and have retained their bright color. Using a slotted spoon, transfer the strands to a paper towel to drain. Using your fingertips, shape the strands into a nest. Place the nest on a clean paper towel to drain, and continue frying and making nests until you have 6 sweet potato nests.

7. Remove the baked sweet potatoes from their skins. Put the pulp in a mixing bowl. Add the remaining 6 tablespoons of ghee, ¼ teaspoon of allspice, and salt to taste and, using an electric hand mixer, beat until very light and fluffy. Scrape the potatoes into a medium nonstick saucepan and place over very low heat. Loosely cover and cook, stirring frequently, for about 5 minutes, or until very hot. Turn off the heat, but leave the pan on the burner to keep them warm while you prepare the duck.

8. Heat the remaining 3 tablespoons of oil in a large sauté pan over medium-high heat. When very hot but not smoking, add the seasoned duck breasts and sear, turning occasionally, for about 8 minutes, or until the breasts are rare in the center. Remove from the pan and allow to rest for a minute. Using a sharp chef's knife, cut each breast on the bias into ¼-inch-thick slices. Keep the slices of each breast together.

9. Spoon equal portions of the sweet potato confit in the center of each of six dinner plates. Fan the duck breast slices so that they radiate from each potato mound. Spoon equal portions of sauce around each breast and around the edge of each plate. Nestle a sweet potato nest on top of the duck. Garnish with a chervil sprig and serve.

Note: You can do a lot of the preparation for this dish ahead of time. Early in the day, the duck breasts can be spiced and marinated, the sauce made, sweet potato strands prepared, and sweet potato confit made. Before dinner, the sauce and sweet potato confit can be reheated, the sweet potato nests made, and the duck breasts cooked.

Wine Suggestions: Bonny Doon Le Cigar Volant
Buehler Zinfandel

Supreme of Pheasant
with Basmati-Truffle Risotto

Serves 6

1 tablespoon black cumin seeds

10 whole cloves

4 cardamom pods

One 3-inch cinnamon stick

$^1/_2$ cup plain nonfat yogurt

1 teaspoon minced fresh ginger

1 teaspoon minced garlic

Coarse salt, to taste

6 pheasant breasts

8 tablespoons (1 stick) butter,
    softened

$^1/_2$ cup finely chopped shallots

2 cups chicken stock

$^1/_2$ cup dry white wine

$^1/_4$ cup peeled, seeded, and finely
    diced plum tomatoes

Freshly ground white pepper, to taste

6 tablespoons ghee (see page 15)

6 tablespoons clam juice

2 tablespoons fresh lemon juice

Pinch of saffron

2 cups cooked basmati rice

$^1/_4$ cup julienned curry leaf

$^1/_4$ cup peanut oil

$^1/_4$ cup shaved white truffles (see
    Note)

6 sprigs fresh chervil

Pheasant is easily overcooked and is often quite dry. I have used an aromatic yogurt marinade to ensure that the pheasant meat remains moist. Unlike a traditional Italian risotto, which requires that the liquid be slowly incorporated, I have made a quick-and-easy basmati rice risotto. Since white truffles lose their perfume and much of their taste when cooked, I add them just before serving, so that their aroma can embrace the diner. All together, we have quite an international dish!

1. Put the black cumin seeds, cloves, cardamom, and cinnamon stick in a small sauté pan over medium heat. Cook, stirring frequently, for about 3 minutes, or until the spices are toasted and aromatic. Remove from the heat and allow to cool slightly. Transfer to a spice grinder and process to a fine powder.

2. Combine the yogurt, ginger, garlic, and salt in a small bowl. Stir in the powdered spices.

3. Place the pheasant breasts in a shallow baking dish. Spread the yogurt mixture over the breasts and allow them to marinate for at least 30 minutes, but no more than 4 hours.

4. Heat 2 tablespoons of the softened butter in a medium saucepan over medium heat. Add the shallots and sauté for 3 minutes. Add the chicken stock, wine, tomatoes, and salt and white pepper to taste. Bring to a simmer. Whisk in the remaining butter and, when well incorporated, lower the heat and cook, stirring frequently, for about 15 minutes, or until the sauce coats the back of a spoon. Pour into the top half of a

double boiler set over boiling water. Cover loosely and keep warm.

5. Combine the ghee, clam juice, lemon juice, and saffron in a medium saucepan over medium heat. Cook for 2 minutes. Stir in the rice and julienned curry leaves. Cover the pan and turn off the heat. Leave the pan on the burner to keep the risotto warm while you cook the pheasant.

6. Heat the peanut oil in a large sauté pan over medium-high heat. Wipe the excess yogurt mixture from the pheasant. Place the pheasant breasts in the pan and cook, turning frequently, for about 10 minutes, or until the meat is cooked through. (Pheasant toughens very quickly, so do not overcook.)

7. Working quickly, toss one half of the truffles into the risotto. Place an equal portion of the risotto into the center of each of 6 dinner plates. Place a pheasant breast on top of the risotto. Drizzle some sauce over the pheasant and around the plate. Sprinkle the remaining truffles over each serving and garnish the pheasant with a sprig of chervil. Serve immediately.

Note: You will be forgiven if you eliminate the truffles. If you do, sauté some wild mushrooms and use them in place of the truffles.

Wine Suggestions: Castello Banfi Brunello
Fortant Cabernet Sauvignon Reserve
The elegantly dry yet hearty-robust flavor of either of these wines is the perfect complement to the richness of the pheasant.

Venison Racks with Indian Grits and Sun-Dried Tomato Chutney

Serves 6

½ cup sun-dried tomatoes (not packed in oil)

1 ancho chile

½ cup plus 6 tablespoons olive oil

2 tablespoons *urad dal*

1 teaspoon cumin seeds

1 tablespoon plus 1 teaspoon mustard seeds

¼ teaspoon toasted ground fenugreek

¼ teaspoon toasted ground asafetida

Six 8-ounce venison chops

12 plum tomatoes, halved and seeded

1 teaspoon ground cumin

6 cups water

Coarse salt, to taste

6 tablespoons ghee (see page 15)

2 cups fine quality grits

6 sprigs fresh rosemary

I've combined flavors from all over the world for this dish. Sun-dried tomatoes and rosemary sing of Italy, grits shout the American South, spices burst forth from India, and the ancho chile is right at home in Mexico. Somehow, all these flavors fuse together to add intensity to the rich meaty flavor of the venison without overpowering it.

1. Combine the sun-dried tomatoes, chile, and ¼ cup of the olive oil in a small bowl. Allow to marinate for 2 hours. Drain well, reserving the tomatoes, chile, and oil in separate dishes.
2. Put the reserved oil in a medium sauté pan over medium heat. Add the *urad dal*, cumin seeds, and 1 teaspoon of the mustard seeds. Cook, stirring constantly, for about 3 minutes, or until the spices begin to brown. Immediately add the fenugreek and asafetida. Remove from the heat and stir in the reserved sun-dried tomatoes and chile. Put the mixture in a food processor fitted with the metal blade and process to a thick paste. Taste and adjust the seasoning with salt. Rub the paste generously on the venison chops. Place them on a plate, lightly cover with plastic film, and let marinate for at least 30 minutes.
3. Preheat the oven to 300°F.
4. Toss the plum tomatoes with ¼ cup of the remaining olive oil in a shallow baking dish. Roast in the oven for 1 hour. Remove from the oven and allow to cool.
5. Put the baked plum tomatoes, ground cumin, 1 cup of the

water, and salt in a blender. Process until very smooth. Pour into a nonreactive container and set aside.

6. Heat 2 tablespoons of ghee in a medium saucepan over medium heat. Add the remaining mustard seeds and sauté for 2 minutes, or until the seeds start to pop. Add the remaining water and bring to a boil. Stir in the grits and remaining ghee. Cover and cook, stirring occasionally, for 15 minutes, or until the grits are thick. Turn off the heat but leave the pan on the burner to keep the grits warm.

7. Preheat the oven to 400°F.

8. Pour the remaining olive oil in a large ovenproof sauté pan over high heat. When hot, but not smoking, add the seasoned venison chops. Sear, turning once, for about 6 minutes, or until the chops are nicely crusted. Roast in the oven for about 8 minutes for medium-rare.

9. Spoon an equal portion of the roasted tomato sauce into the center of each of 6 dinner plates. Spoon some of the grits into the center of the sauce on each plate. Place a venison chop on top of the grits. Garnish with a sprig of rosemary and serve.

Wine Suggestions: Chapoutier Crozes-Hermitage
Black Opal Shiraz
The earthy spiciness of either of these red wines is a marvelous match for this highly flavored dish.

Antelope Chops
with Blackberry-Ginger Chutney

Serves 6

$^1/_2$ cup plus 6 tablespoons olive oil

1 teaspoon mustard seeds

1 cup blackberries, well washed, picked clean of stems, and drained (see Note)

2 teaspoons fresh ginger juice (see page 12)

Pinch of ground turmeric

Coarse salt, to taste

6 tablespoons *dhana dal* (see Note)

6 tablespoons toasted cracked black pepper

1 cup fresh basil leaves

Six 8-ounce antelope chops (see Note)

3 cups peanut oil (approximately)

Eighteen $^1/_2$-inch-thick slices Japanese eggplant (about 4 eggplant)

6 sprigs fresh herbs (optional)

In this recipe, I use *dhana dal* in the rub. It has a lovely delicate corianderlike flavor that accents the meat beautifully and makes a good counterpoint to the chutney. I add a bit of zest to the already rich fruity flavor of the blackberries, which I think makes the chutney a perfect foil for the game.

1. Heat 6 tablespoons of the olive oil in a medium sauté pan over medium heat. Add the mustard seeds and cook, stirring frequently, for about 3 minutes, or until the seeds begin to pop. Stir in the blackberries, ginger juice, turmeric, and salt. Cook, stirring frequently, for about 5 minutes, or until the berries are quite soft. Turn off the heat. Cover and leave the pan on the burner to keep the chutney barely warm.

2. Put the *dhana dal* in a small sauté pan over medium heat. Cook, stirring frequently, for about 3 minutes or until the dal is nicely toasted. Remove from the heat and cool slightly. Transfer to a spice grinder and process until finely ground.

3. Combine the ground *dal* with the cracked pepper and $^1/_4$ cup of the remaining olive oil. Add salt to taste and stir to blend.

4. Working with about 8 leaves at a time, stack the basil leaves, one on top of the other, and then roll them up, cigar fashion. Cut each roll, crosswise, into $^1/_4$-inch pieces. (These ragged strips are called a chiffonade.) Set aside.

5. Preheat the oven to 400°F.

6. Generously coat the chops with the dal mixture. Place on a plate and lightly cover with plastic film.

7. Heat the remaining ¼ cup of olive oil in a large ovenproof sauté pan over medium-high heat. Put the chops in the pan and sear, turning once, for about 5 minutes, or until the chops are nicely crusted. Roast in the oven for about 10 minutes, or until the chops are medium-rare.

8. While the chops are cooking, prepare the eggplant. Heat the peanut oil in a deep-fat fryer until it registers 365°F on a candy thermometer. Add the eggplant, a few slices at a time, and fry for about 3 minutes, or until the eggplant is cooked and golden. Place on a paper towel to drain. Season to taste with salt. Continue frying until all of the slices are cooked. Place the eggplant in a shallow dish and gently toss it with the reserved basil chiffonade.

9. Spoon an equal portion of the blackberry-ginger chutney into the center of each of 6 dinner plates. Stack 3 slices of eggplant on each plate, allowing the stacks to be slightly out of line. Lean a chop into each stack. Garnish with an herb sprig and serve.

Note: The fresh blackberries may be replaced with frozen blackberries with no loss of flavor.
Dhana dal is a split coriander seed that is available in East Indian and Pakistani markets.
Venison or lamb chops or a beefsteak can be used insead of the antelope chops. If the weather permits, the chops could easily be cooked on a grill.

Wine Suggestions: Château Gloria St.-Julien
Columbia Syrah
This rich game dish demands a sturdy dry red wine, which you will find in either of these bottles.

Fish

Golden Trout with Ginger-Fennel Vinaigrette

Provençal Herb–Seared Salmon with Sweet Carrot
  Confit

Fillet of Salmon with Dill and Turmeric Emulsion

Swordfish Fillet with Cilantro Vinaigrette and
  Stewed Tomatoes

Swordfish Rubbed with Tamarind-Ginger Chutney

Opakapaka with Mango-Papaya Salsa

Grouper with Mango-Jalapeño Sauce

Spice-Crusted Tuna with Tamarind Seaweed Rolls

Halibut with Lime-Leek Beurre Blanc and
  Cauliflower Bouquets

Fillet of Sea Bass with Madras Curry Masala

Red Snapper with Garlic, Cumin, and Purple
  Potatoes

Dover Sole with Curry Leaf Emulsion

Golden Trout
with Ginger-Fennel Vinaigrette

Serves 6

¹/₄ cup fennel seeds, crushed

2 tablespoons minced fresh ginger

6 tablespoons dry white wine

6 tablespoons extra virgin olive oil

6 boneless whole golden trout (other trout can be substituted)

12 large fresh rosemary branches

3 tablespoons ghee (see page 15)

3 cups ¹/₂-inch dice zucchini

Coarse salt and freshly ground black pepper to taste

Although I infrequently use extra virgin olive oil, this dish requires its heady aroma and intense color. The palette of this plate speaks overwhelmingly of the South of France.

1. Preheat the oven to 500°F.

2. Put the fennel seeds and ginger in a blender or mini–food processor and blend well. Spoon out about one half of the mixture and set it aside. Add the wine, and with the motor running, pour in the olive oil and process until well emulsified. Strain through a fine sieve into a nonreactive container and set aside.

3. Put 2 rosemary branches into the cavity of each fish. Rub both sides of the fish with some of the reserved ginger-fennel vinaigrette. Place on a low-sided baking sheet lined with parchment paper. Drizzle the fish with 2 tablespoons of ghee.

4. Roast the fish in the oven for about 5 minutes, or until the skin has crisped and the fish is cooked through.

5. While the fish is roasting, heat the remaining ghee in a medium sauté pan over medium-high heat. Add the zucchini and sauté for 3 minutes, or until heated through but still firm. Season with salt and pepper. Set aside and keep warm.

6. Place a trout across the center of each of 6 dinner plates. Drizzle the reserved vinaigrette over the top of each fish and spoon a portion of zucchini under the tail end.

Wine Suggestions: Pine Ridge Chardonnay
La Forêt Mâcon Villages

Provençal Herb–Seared Salmon with Sweet Carrot Confit

Serves 6

2 pounds carrots, peeled and
    quartered
Coarse salt, to taste
Pinch saffron threads
12 tablespoons (1 ½ sticks) unsalted
    butter, cut into small pieces
Freshly ground white pepper, to taste
½ cup herbes de Provence (see Note)
Six 5-ounce skinless salmon fillets
2 tablespoons ghee (see page 15)

This is one of my favorite dishes, perhaps because it pairs well with so many different wines. It is also very simple to prepare. However, I must warn you that the carrot confit, which I learned from Alain Passard (of Restaurant Arpege), is extremely rich and buttery. For a once-in-awhile treat, it turns a simple meal into a feast. If the confit is too rich for you, the herb-scented salmon could easily be thrown on the grill and then served with a green salad and some crusty peasant bread, for an entirely different taste sensation.

1. Put the carrots and cold salted water to cover in a medium saucepan over high heat. Bring to a boil. Lower the heat and simmer for about 10 minutes, or until the carrots are very tender. Drain well, reserving about ½ of the cooking water. Place the carrots and saffron in a food processor fitted with the metal blade and process until very smooth, adding some of the cooking water, if necessary, to make a smooth puree.

2. Transfer the carrot puree to a medium nonstick sauté pan over medium-low heat. When the carrots are hot, begin beating in the butter, a bit at a time. When all of the butter has been incorporated, taste and adjust the seasoning with salt and white pepper. Remove from the heat. Cover the confit, and keep warm.

3. Put the *herbes de Provence* in a shallow bowl. One at a time, place the salmon fillets into the *herbes*, turning to generously coat each side.

4. Heat the ghee in a large nonstick sauté pan over high heat. Add the seasoned salmon fillets, working in batches if necessary, and sear for about 3 minutes. Turn and sear the other sides for 3 minutes, or just until the salmon is still slightly rare in the center.

5. Spoon a pool of carrot confit in the bottom of each of 6 shallow soup bowls. Place a piece of salmon in the center and serve.

Note: I make my own herbes de Provence *by combining equal amounts of dried basil, lavender, thyme, summer savory, marjoram, rosemary, and fennel seeds. However, you can purchase a ready-made blend in most supermarkets and specialty food stores. In France, this classic mixture is usually packed in charming little clay pots with a piece of colorful Provençal fabric tied over the top.*

Wine Suggestions: Coche-Dury Bourgogne Grand Ordinare
David Bruce Pinot Noir
The sweet, cherry qualities of Pinot Noir are the perfect touch to bring out the full rich flavor of this very rich dish.

Fillet of Salmon
with Dill and Turmeric Emulsion

Serves 6

Six 6-ounce skinless salmon fillets
1 large bunch fresh dill, well washed,
  stems removed
1 teaspoon ground turmeric
1/4 cup plus 2 teaspoons olive oil
1/4 cup fresh lemon juice
Coarse salt, to taste
24 baby carrots with tops

As you may have noticed, I love the combination of flavors and colors when salmon is highlighted with carrots. This is an extremely simple recipe, yet it is almost earthshaking in its perfume. I think it is a perfect illustration of how the right combination of ingredients makes a dish special. The sweet baby carrots are soft accents for the heady emulsion and color of the salmon.

1. Place the salmon fillets in a shallow, nonreactive baking dish.
2. Put the dill and turmeric in a blender. Add 1/4 cup of the olive oil, begin processing, and with the motor running, add the lemon juice and salt. Continue processing until the mixture is well blended. Divide the emulsion in half. Pour one half into a small bowl and use it to generously coat the salmon fillets, discarding any leftover emulsion. Cover with plastic film and allow to marinate for 30 minutes. (The fillets can marinate for up to 12 hours, covered and refrigerated. Bring to room temperature before cooking.) Set remaining emulsion aside.
3. Scrub the carrots under cool running water. Remove all but about 1 inch of the green tops. Gently peel the carrots, being careful to remove as little flesh as possible. (Often the skin of baby carrots is so fine that if you scrub them well, you will not have to peel them at all.) Put the carrots in a large saucepan filled with boiling water to cover, and blanch for about 1 minute over high heat. Drain well and refresh in cold running water. When cool, pat dry and set aside.

4. Preheat the oven to 400°F.

5. Place a large nonstick ovenproof sauté pan over medium-high heat. Carefully lay the marinated fillets in the pan, taking care not to crowd them. Sear for about 2 minutes, or until the bottom of each fillet is lightly browned. Turn and sear the other side for 1 minute. Roast in the oven for about 8 minutes, or until the salmon has set but is still moist in the center.

6. While the salmon is roasting, heat the remaining olive oil in a large sauté pan over medium-high heat. Add the carrots and sauté for about 3 minutes, or until just heated through. Season with salt.

7. Place a salmon fillet in the center of each of 6 dinner plates. Arrange 4 carrots alongside each fillet. Drizzle an equal portion of the remaining half of emulsion over each fillet and around the plate and serve.

Wine Suggestions: Merryvale Starmont Chardonnay
Robert Mondavi Reserve Chardonnay
A buttery, richly oaked Chardonnay blends extremely well with the high-fat, softly textured salmon fillet.

Swordfish Fillet with Cilantro Vinaigrette and Stewed Tomatoes

Serves 6

1 serrano chile, stemmed and seeded

$1/4$ cup fresh cilantro leaves, plus 6 sprigs for garnish

$1/8$ teaspoon toasted cumin seeds

2 tablespoons canola oil

2 tablespoons dry white wine

1 tablespoon balsamic vinegar

Coarse salt, to taste

1 tablespoon olive oil

6 very ripe medium tomatoes, peeled, cored, seeded, and chopped

1 tablespoon unsalted butter

$1 1/2$ pounds swordfish steak, cut 1 - inch thick, divided into 6 equal pieces

Freshly ground black pepper, to taste

3 tablespoons ghee (see page 15)

The vinaigrette I use in this dish is extremely zesty and aromatic, but the dense, meaty swordfish can more than stand up to it. The sweet tomatoes are a great counterbalance to this very colorful plate.

1. Put the chile, cilantro leaves, cumin seeds, canola oil, wine, vinegar, and salt in a blender. Process until very smooth. Remove from the blender and set aside.

2. Heat the olive oil in a nonstick sauté pan over medium heat. Add the tomatoes and salt to taste. Cook, stirring occasionally, for about 5 minutes, or until the tomatoes are very soft and the juices have thickened slightly. Stir in the butter. When well incorporated, remove from the heat and keep warm.

3. Season the swordfish with salt and pepper. Heat 2 tablespoons of the ghee in a nonstick sauté pan over high heat. When very hot, but not smoking, add the swordfish. Sear for 4 minutes, then turn and sear the other side for 3 minutes, or just until the fish is firm to the touch. Do not overcook.

4. Place an equal portion of the stewed tomatoes in the bottom of each of 6 shallow soup bowls, mounding the tomatoes slightly in the center. Place a piece of swordfish in the center of the tomatoes. Using a pastry brush, lightly brush the top of the fish with the remaining ghee. Drizzle the vinaigrette over the entire dish. Place a cilantro sprig into the fish and serve.

Note: Halibut, cod, or lobster would also work well in this dish.
If your tomatoes are not intensely sweet, add a pinch of sugar or a few

drops of maple syrup to counteract the pungent vinaigrette. In a pinch, you could also use imported canned Italian plum tomatoes instead of fresh ones.

Wine Suggestions: Louis Jadot Savigny-Les-Beaune Les Dominaudes
Au Bon Climat Santa Barbara Pinot Noir
Because swordfish is a meaty fish and is combined here with tomatoes for a full-bodied dish, we like to serve a red wine. The sweetness and fruity acid of Pinot Noir makes it the perfect wine for this dish.

Swordfish Rubbed with Tamarind-Ginger Chutney

Serves 6

3 tablespoons canola oil

2 tablespoons *urad dal* (see Note)

1 teaspoon mustard seeds

1 teaspoon cumin seeds

2 dried cayenne chiles

1/2 cup tamarind pulp (see page 18)

1/4 cup coarsely chopped fresh ginger

2 tablespoons jaggery (see page 18)

Coarse salt, to taste

1 1/2 pounds swordfish steak, cut
   1- inch thick, divided into 6 equal
   pieces

Spinach Puree (recipe follows)

Fried Leek Nests (recipe follows)

12 chives (optional)

6 edible flowers: pansies,
   nasturtiums, and so on (optional)

A mosaic of flavors adds complexity to a simple dish: a traditional chutney, a firm meaty fish, an unadorned spinach puree, and a piquant leek garnish. Tamarind-ginger chutney is very Indian and stands up to the rich flavor of the fish. The marinated swordfish would also be terrific cooked on a grill, for an easy summer meal. In that case, serve it with a fresh spinach salad instead.

1. Heat the oil in a medium sauté pan over medium heat. Add the *urad dal* and cook, stirring, for 1 minute. Add the mustard seeds and stir for another minute. Stir in the cumin seeds and sauté for 2 minutes, or until the mixture is very aromatic. Add the chiles, tamarind, and ginger and cook, stirring frequently, for about 3 minutes, or until the ginger has begun to soften. Stir in the jaggery and cook for an additional minute. Scrape into a blender and process until you have a puree. Taste and adjust the seasoning with salt. Allow to cool slightly. (This could be made up to a week in advance; refrigerate in a nonreactive container.)

2. Place the swordfish in a nonreactive dish and generously coat all sides with the tamarind chutney. Cover and marinate for 1 hour in the refrigerator.

3. Preheat the oven to 450°F.

4. Place a large, ovenproof, nonstick sauté pan over medium-high heat. Add the marinated swordfish and sear for 2 minutes per side, or just until golden. Roast in the oven for about 10 minutes, or until the swordfish is firm to the touch.

5. Spoon 3 tablespoons of the spinach puree in the center of each of 6 dinner plates. Lay a swordfish fillet in the center of the puree on each plate. Place a leek nest on top of each piece of fish and serve immediately, garnished with chives and edible flowers.

Spinach Puree

3 pounds fresh spinach, well washed
   and stemmed
3 tablespoons canola oil
1 teaspoon minced garlic
Coarse salt, to taste

1. Wash spinach thoroughly. Spin or pat dry.
2. Heat the oil in a large sauté pan over medium heat. Add the garlic and sauté for 1 minute. Stir in the spinach, a bit at a time, and sauté for about 3 minutes or until it is wilted.
3. Scrape the spinach into a blender or food processor fitted with the metal blade. Add salt to taste and process until spinach is a thick puree. (This may be done a day or two in advance of use. If so, place in a nonreactive container, cover, and refrigerate until ready to use).
4. Scrape the spinach puree into a nonstick saucepan and place over very low heat to keep warm until ready to serve.
5. Serve as directed above or as a side dish.

Fried Leek Nests

3 leeks
4 cups vegetable oil (approximately)
Pinch ground cumin
Coarse salt, to taste

1. Trim the leeks of all but 1 inch of the green part; wash thoroughly. Cut lengthwise into a fine julienne. Pat dry.
2. Lay a large double layer of paper towels on a clean counter.
3. Heat the oil in a deep saucepan or deep-fat fryer over high heat until a candy thermometer registers 360°F. Add the leeks, a few at a time, and fry until golden, but still soft and pliable.
4. Using a slotted spoon, transfer the leeks to the paper towels to drain. When cool enough to handle, use your fingertips to shape the fried leeks into 4 small nestlike shapes. Season with cumin and salt.
5. Transfer the nests to a baking sheet lined with a double layer of paper towels. If the nests cool, put them in a very low oven for a minute or two before serving.

Note: Urad dal is available in Indian, Pakistani, or Middle Eastern markets, at some specialty food stores, or through a mail order source listed on page 209.

Wine Suggestions: Duckhorn Vineyards Merlot
Château Bon Pasteur Pomerol

Opakapaka with Mango-Papaya Salsa

Serves 6

2 tablespoons ghee (see page 15)

7 very large button mushrooms, wiped clean and chopped

1 tablespoon minced shallot

1 tablespoon minced fresh flat-leaf parsley

Coarse salt and freshly ground black pepper, to taste

2 tablespoons minced garlic

$1/2$ teaspoon ground cumin

Pinch dried red chile powder

Six 6-ounce skinless opakapaka fillets (see Note)

1 tablespoon fine quality olive oil

Mango-Papaya Salsa (recipe follows)

12 fresh chives

When I participated in the "Cuisines of the Sun" event in Hawaii, I was introduced to this marvelous fish. Its delicate flavor seemed to capture the essence of Hawaii on the plate. Here, it becomes part of a classic fusion recipe. I begin with a mushroom duxelles from the French repertoire. Then I season the Hawaiian fish with just a hint of Indian spice and give an exciting finish to the plate with a wonderfully light and refreshing fruit-based salsa.

1. Preheat the oven to 450°F.

2. Place 1 tablespoon of ghee in a medium nonstick sauté pan over medium heat. Add the mushrooms, shallot, and parsley. Sauté for about 5 minutes, or until the mushrooms have exuded most of their liquid and the mixture is well blended. Season with salt and pepper. Remove from the heat and tent lightly with aluminum foil to keep warm.

3. Combine the garlic, cumin, and chile powder with salt to taste in a small bowl. Set aside.

4. Using a paper towel, pat the fish dry. Rub each fish fillet with an equal amount of the garlic mixture. Lightly drizzle olive oil over the top.

5. Heat the remaining tablespoon of ghee in a large nonstick, ovenproof sauté pan over high heat. When very hot, but not smoking, add the fish and sear for 1 minute. Turn and sear the other side for 30 seconds. Remove from the heat immediately and place in the oven. Roast for about 4 minutes, or just until the fish is opaque.

6. Place an equal portion of the mushroom duxelles in the center of each of 6 luncheon plates. Place an opakapaka fillet on top of the mushrooms. Spoon some mango-papaya salsa over the fish and generously drizzle salsa around the edge of each plate. Serve immediately.

Mango-Papaya Salsa

1 large green mango
2 medium ripe papayas
1 small red onion
1 jalapeño chile, stemmed, seeded, and minced
10 fresh curry leaves, julienned
1/2 teaspoon ground cumin
3 tablespoons extra virgin olive oil
1 teaspoon fresh ginger juice (see page 14)
Coarse salt, to taste

1. Peel the mango and cut it into 1/4-inch dice. Place in a large nonreactive bowl.
2. Peel and seed the papayas. Cut them into 1/4-inch dice and add them to the mango.
3. Peel the onion and cut it into 1/4-inch dice. Add it to the mango-papaya mixture, along with the jalapeño, curry leaves, and cumin. Toss to mix well.
4. Add the oil and ginger juice. Season with salt and allow to marinate at room temperature for 30 minutes before serving.

Note: Opakapaka is a rather fatty gray-and-pink snapper highly prized in Hawaii for sashimi. If unavailable in your area, you can substitute a local snapper or any other firm-textured, delicately flavored fish.
The salsa may be made 1 day prior to using and stored, covered, in the refrigerator.

Wine Suggestions: Hugel Gewürztraminer
Geyser Peak Gewürztraminer
A fruity, spicy Gewürz nicely handles the fish and fruit.

Grouper with Mango-Jalapeño Sauce

Six 6-ounce skinless grouper fillets
1 teaspoon ground coriander seeds
Coarse salt, to taste
2 tablespoons olive oil
1 teaspoon mustard seeds
6 cups finely shredded cabbage
Mango-Jalapeño Sauce (recipe
   follows)

The skin of a grouper has an extremely strong flavor, so it should always be removed before cooking. The flesh is very lean but firm, which makes it almost foolproof in the kitchen. I use grouper often both for its flavor and because it is readily available from Florida waters. Grouper is a subspecies of sea bass, so if you can't find it, use any bass instead.

1. Preheat the oven to 400°F.

2. Season the grouper fillets with the coriander and salt. Place a large nonstick, ovenproof skillet over medium-high heat. Add the seasoned grouper and sear for about 2 minutes, or until the bottom of each fillet is lightly browned. Turn and sear the other side. Roast in the oven for about 10 minutes, or until the fish is set but still moist in the center.

3. While the fish is roasting, heat the oil in a large sauté pan over high heat. Add the mustard seeds and cook, stirring constantly, for about 2 minutes, or until the seeds begin to pop. Add the cabbage and sauté for about 4 minutes, or just until the cabbage begins to wilt. Remove immediately from the heat. Tent the cabbage lightly with foil to keep warm.

4. Divide the cabbage among 6 dinner plates. Place a grouper fillet on top of each portion. Drizzle some of the Mango-Jalapeño Sauce over the fish and around the edge of the plate and serve.

Mangoes need very strong sun to bring out their profound sweetness, and India certainly provides that! Canned Indian mangoes, available in Indian and Asian markets, have such an intense sweetness that once you have used them in sauces and desserts, you will never be without them. I usually puree the mangoes as soon as I open the can as I never use them whole or in pieces. Any leftover puree can be frozen. This is one of the very few commercially prepared products that I use in the kitchen.

Mango-Jalapeño Sauce

2 cups pureed canned Indian
   mangoes
1 jalapeño chile, stemmed, seeded,
   and chopped or to taste
1/3 cup fine quality olive oil
1 tablespoon fresh lime juice
   (approximately)

Pour the mango puree in a blender and add the chile. Process until very smooth. Slowly add the oil and blend until well incorporated. Taste and adjust the flavor with lime juice. Pour into a squeeze bottle and refrigerate until ready to use. Sauce keeps up to a week.

Wine Suggestions: Château de Fieuzal Graves
Frog's Leap Sauvignon Blanc
A Sauvignon Blanc–based wine will enhance the complex yet cool spiciness of this dish.

Spice-Crusted Tuna
with Tamarind Seaweed Rolls

Serves 6

2 tablespoons coriander seeds

3 tablespoons urad dal (see Note)

2 dried cayenne chiles

1 tablespoon mustard seeds

1 tablespoon cumin seeds

1/4 cup black sesame seeds

3/4 cup short-grain sticky rice, well
washed and drained

1 cup boiling water

1/4 cup tamarind pulp (see page 18)

15 fresh curry leaves, julienned

1 tablespoon ground turmeric

Coarse salt, to taste

6 tablespoons canola oil

6 sheets nori, 3 x 8 inches (see Note)

1 1/2 pounds tuna steak, cut into six 6-
ounce triangles

Roasted Tomato Vinaigrette (recipe
follows)

Traditional sushi contains no spices and relies on the purity of the ingredients to make its statement. I wanted to use spices as a complement to the lightly seared sushi-grade tuna in this recipe. The two layers of seasoning, first the spice mixture, and then the delicate black sesame seed powder, react wonderfully on the palate and create a lovely, rather subtle bouquet. So much of this recipe can be done ahead of time that it's a snap to make for guests.

1. Put the coriander in a small nonstick frying pan over medium heat. Toast, stirring frequently, for 1 minute. Add the *urad dal* and toast for an additional 30 seconds. Stir in the chiles and then the mustard seeds. Cook for 1 minute. Add the cumin seeds and continue to cook, stirring frequently, for about 2 additional minutes or until the seeds are toasted and the mixture is very aromatic. Transfer to a spice grinder and grind into a very fine powder. Set aside, reserving 2 tablespoons separately.

2. Put the black sesame seeds in a small frying pan over medium heat. Cook, stirring frequently, for about 3 minutes, or until the seeds are lightly toasted. Transfer to the spice grinder and grind into a very fine powder. (It is important that the powder be very fine so that it will adhere to the spice mixture on the tuna, to make a fine outer coating.) Set aside, reserving 1 tablespoon separately.

3. Put the rice in a heavy-bottomed saucepan with a tight fitting lid. Add the boiling water and place over medium-high heat.

Cover and bring to a boil. Lower the heat and cook for 15 minutes, or until the water has been absorbed and the rice is soft and slightly sticky.

4. Put the cooked rice in a nonreactive mixing bowl. Stir in the tamarind, curry leaves, turmeric, salt, 2 tablespoons of the oil, the reserved 2 tablespoons of spice mixture, and the reserved 1 tablespoon of toasted sesame seed powder. Gently mix well, but do not mash the rice grains.

5. Lay the nori sheets out on a clean counter. Using a pastry brush, lightly moisten each sheet with cold water. With wet fingers, spread an equal portion of the rice mixture onto each nori sheet. Roll tightly to make a neat firm rice roll. Place the rolls on a plate, cover lightly, and set aside.

6. Clean the tuna pieces of any blood or cartilage. Pat dry.

7. Place the tuna in a shallow nonreactive dish. Generously sprinkle each piece with the remaining spice mixture, making sure that you coat all surfaces.

8. Put the remaining black sesame seed powder in a clean shallow dish. One at a time, coat each spiced tuna piece with the sesame powder.

9. Heat the remaining oil in a large sauté pan over medium-high heat. Add the tuna pieces and sear about 3 1/2 minutes per side for medium-rare.

10. Spoon 2 tablespoons of the tomato vinaigrette into the center of each of 6 dinner plates, pushing out with the back of a spoon to make a neat circle. Lay a piece of tuna in the center of each vinaigrette circle. Place a rice roll next to the tuna and serve.

Roasted Tomato Vinaigrette

10 very ripe plum tomatoes
1/4 cup dry white wine
1/4 cup peanut oil
Coarse salt, to taste

1. Preheat the oven to 350°F.

2. Wash and dry the tomatoes, and place them in a shallow baking dish. Roast them in the oven for about 30 minutes, or until lightly browned and very soft. Remove from the heat and cool slightly.

3. Slip off the skins, core, and squeeze out the seeds.

4. Put the tomatoes in a blender. Begin to process, adding the wine and then the oil with the motor running. Taste and adjust seasoning with salt. Cover and set aside until ready to use.

Note: Urad dal *is available at Indian, Pakistani, or Middle Eastern markets, at some specialty food stores, or through a mail order source listed on page 209.*

Nori are paper-thin sheets of dried seaweed, available from Japanese markets, specialty food stores, or by mail order from one of the sources listed on page 209.

The spice mixture and sesame seed powder can be made a few days ahead and stored, tightly covered. The vinaigrette can be made up to 3 days in advance and stored, covered, in the refrigerator. Finally, the rice rolls can be prepared early in the day, wrapped in plastic film, and stored in the refrigerator until ready to serve.

Wine Suggestions: Château St. Jean Chardonnay
La Chablisienne
A very dry Chardonnay with vibrant acidity is the perfect choice for the highly spiced seared tuna.

Halibut with Lime-Leek Beurre Blanc and Cauliflower Bouquets

Serves 6

1 head cauliflower

1 lime

1 leek

¼ cup ghee (see page 15)

1 jalapeño chile, stemmed and chopped

1 ¼ teaspoons ajowan

¼ cup water

1 cup heavy cream

4 tablespoons (½ stick) butter, softened

Coarse salt, to taste

6 tablespoons canola oil

Six 6-ounce halibut filets

6 to 12 small leaves radicchio di Treviso (a deep dark red Italian salad chicory, optional)

Cauliflower is very common in Indian cooking—it seems to lend itself to many different types of preparation. Here we have a classic beurre blanc made not so classic with the addition of chile and *ajowan*. The flavor and delicacy of the butter-laden sauce balances the low-fat halibut beautifully. I think this is a perfect fusion match.

1. Wash the cauliflower well. Break the top into very small florets, discarding the stems. (Or save them for a cream soup base.) Pat dry and set aside.

2. Remove all the peel, pith, membrane, and any seeds from the lime. Cut the lime into small dice. Set aside.

3. Trim the leek of all but about 1 inch of the green part. Cut it in half lengthwise and wash well under cold running water. Pat dry and finely chop.

4. Heat the ghee in a small saucepan over medium heat. Add the reserved lime and leek along with the chile and ¼ teaspoon of the *ajowan*. Stir to combine. Add the water and bring to a boil. Lower the heat and simmer for 5 minutes.

5. Scrape the leek and lime mixture into a blender and process until smooth. Pour through a fine strainer into a clean small saucepan. Place over medium heat and whisk in the cream. Bring to a simmer. Lower the heat immediately and allow the mixture to barely simmer for 10 minutes, or until slightly reduced. Rapidly whisk in the softened butter and continue cooking at a low simmer for an additional 10 minutes, or until

the beurre blanc is a slightly thick, uniform sauce. Taste and adjust seasoning with salt, if necessary. Cover lightly and place over a pan of hot water to keep warm until ready to use.

6. Heat 3 tablespoons of canola oil in a medium sauté pan over medium heat. Add the reserved cauliflower and sauté for about 5 minutes, or until the cauliflower is crisp-tender. Tent lightly with aluminum foil and set aside to keep warm.

7. Heat the remaining oil in a large sauté pan over medium-high heat. Add the halibut fillets and sear for 4 minutes per side, or just until the fish is firm to the touch and the outsides are golden brown. Sprinkle with salt and the remaining *ajowan*.

8. Spoon a pool of lime-leek beurre blanc into the center of each of 6 dinner plates. Place a halibut fillet at a slight angle in the middle of each plate. Place 2 cauliflower florets on top of the fish and, if desired, garnish with 1 or 2 leaves of radicchio Treviso.

Wine Suggestions: Zind-Humbrecht Riesling
F. E. Trimbach Riesling
A steely, austere Riesling from Alsace goes extremely well with the mildly flavored halibut and its subtly aromatic accompaniments.

Fillet of Sea Bass
with Madras Curry Masala

Serves 6

2 teaspoons coriander seeds

2 teaspoons cumin seeds

2 teaspoons mustard seeds

20 black peppercorns

4 whole cloves

3 medium dried cayenne chiles

Pinch ground cinnamon

1/2 cup freshly grated coconut (see Note)

1/2 cup plus 2 tablespoons canola oil

Coarse salt, to taste

Six 6-ounce skinless sea bass fillets

6 cups fresh spinach leaves, well washed

Ordinarily I would choose something other than the Indian buzz-word *masala* as the name of a dish, but this recipe transports me back to my childhood and family vacations in Madras, so Madras Curry Masala it is. In Madras, we would often dine in pristine little cottage-style restaurants, where the food was prepared as if for the gods. My father, a fanatic for cleanliness (which he felt was perhaps even higher than godliness), particularly relished these meals because they were created in what he considered to be spotless surroundings. Here, then, is my recollection of those Madras meals.

1. Place a small nonstick sauté pan over medium heat. Add the coriander seeds and cook, stirring frequently, for about 2 minutes, or until fragrant. Add the cumin and mustard seeds, the peppercorns, cloves, and chiles. Cook for about an additional 3 minutes, or until the spices begin to color and are very aromatic. Remove from the pan and allow to cool. Put in a spice grinder and process until quite fine. Transfer to a small bowl and stir in the cinnamon.

2. Put the coconut in a blender. Add the spice mixture and, with the motor running, slowly add about 1/2 cup of oil. Process until the mixture is moist and well blended. Taste and adjust the seasoning with salt.

3. Preheat the oven to 400°F.

4. Generously coat the sea bass fillets with the spice mixture. Using a pastry brush, lightly coat them with 1 tablespoon of the remaining oil.

5. Place a large nonstick, ovenproof sauté pan over medium-high heat. When very hot but not smoking, add the fish, being careful not to crowd the pan. Sear for 2 minutes, or until the bottom is nicely browned. Turn and sear the other side for 1 minute. Roast in the oven and for about 10 minutes, or until the fish is set but still moist in the center.

6. While the fish is roasting, heat the remaining oil in a large nonstick sauté pan over medium-high heat. Add the spinach and sauté for about 3 minutes, or until it just begins to wilt. Remove immediately from the heat.

7. Place an equal mound of spinach into the center of each of six dinner plates. Place a sea bass fillet on top of each spinach mound and serve.

Note: If you cannot get a fresh coconut, use ¹/₂ cup dried unsweetened coconut moistened with 1/2 cup heavy cream.

Wine Suggestions: Guigal Côte Rôtie Brune Blonde
Qupé Syrah
The exotic pepperiness of the Syrah grape is a wonderful complement to this well-spiced dish.

Red Snapper
with Garlic, Cumin, and Purple Potatoes

Serves 6

1 tablespoon minced garlic

1 tablespoon crushed toasted cumin
    seeds

1 tablespoon dried red chile flakes

$1/4$ teaspoon ground turmeric

Coarse salt, to taste

$1/4$ cup plus 1 tablespoon ghee (see
    page 15)

Six 6-ounce skinless red snapper
    fillets

6 medium purple potatoes

2 tablespoons unsalted butter,
    softened

Freshly ground pepper, to taste

$1/4$ cup fresh lemon juice

6 fresh rosemary branches (optional)

6 edible flowers: pansies,
    nasturtiums, and so on (optional)

Great color! Magnificent flavors! I use the purple Peruvian potatoes for their pale, almost gray color and their distinctive flavor but you can substitute any other firm, moist potato, Yukon golds being a particularly good alternative. This dish is so moist and delicate that I never serve it with a sauce. However, if you feel you would like additional color and zest, you might want to serve it with a cumin-scented tomato coulis (see page 34).

1. In a small bowl, combine the garlic, cumin seeds, chile, turmeric, and salt. Add 1 tablespoon of the ghee to moisten the mixture. Generously coat each snapper fillet with the garlic mixture. Set aside.

2. Put the potatoes and cold salted water to cover in a medium saucepan over high heat. Bring to a boil. Lower the heat and simmer for about 15 minutes, or until the potatoes are tender when pierced with a fork. Drain and peel carefully. (I do not remove the peels before cooking in order to preserve some of the color.) Cut the potatoes into cubes and push through a ricer (or use whatever method you would normally use to mash potatoes). Add the butter and beat until well mashed. Taste and adjust seasoning with salt and pepper. Lightly tent the potatoes with foil to keep warm.

3. Place a large nonstick skillet over medium-high heat. Add the remaining ghee and allow it to just warm. Carefully lay the fillets into the pan, taking care not to crowd. Lower the heat to medium. Cook, turning as necessary, for about 7 minutes, or

until the fillets are nicely browned and firm to the touch, and the ghee has browned slightly but has not burned. You want the browned butter to impart a sweet, nutty taste to the fish.

4. Place 3 tablespoons of the mashed potatoes in the center of each of 6 dinner plates. Place a fillet on top of the potatoes. Drizzle lemon juice over the top and serve with a rosemary branch and an edible flower on top of each fillet, if desired.

Wine Suggestions: Matanzas Creek Chardonnay
Grgich Hills Chardonnay
The structure and profile of either of these richly graceful wines is an extraordinary match for this snapper dish.

Dover Sole with Curry Leaf Emulsion

Serves 6

1/4 cup fresh curry leaves
1/4 cup dry white wine
2 tablespoons balsamic vinegar
1/2 cup plus 2 tablespoons olive oil
Coarse salt, to taste
12 Japanese eggplants
Six 6-ounce Dover sole fillets

You have to be careful with the tropical sensibility of curry leaves (which have nothing to do with curry powder) because they can impart too much of a good thing. I often use them as an accent to add flavor without calories when I do spa cooking. Dover sole isn't always readily available, but if you can find it, I think that you will appreciate its wonderfully delicate flavor. The curry leaf emulsion lends just the right touch of acid to bring out the "soul" of this superb fish!

1. Place the curry leaves, wine, and vinegar in a blender and process until smooth. With the motor running, pour in 1/4 cup of the olive oil. Process until the mixture is emulsified. Taste and adjust seasoning with salt. Set aside.

2. Preheat the oven to 400°F.

3. Wash and dry the eggplants. Trim off the stem end and two of the long sides from each eggplant, so that you can cut 4 equal lengthwise slices from each eggplant, having skin only around the edges.

4. Heat 3 tablespoons of the remaining oil in a large nonstick sauté pan over medium heat. Add the eggplant, a few slices at a time, and cook, turning occasionally, for about 4 minutes, or until they are lightly browned. You may need additional oil to brown all of the slices. Transfer the slices to a baking sheet and when all the slices are brown, roast in the oven for 7 minutes, or until the eggplant is cooked though. Remove from the oven and tent lightly with aluminum foil to keep warm.

5. Heat the remaining oil in a large sauté pan over medium-high heat. Add the sole and cook, turning once, for about 2 minutes per side, or just until the fish is set but still moist in the center.

6. Place 4 slices of eggplant across the center of each of 6 dinner plates. Place a piece of sole on top of the eggplant. Whisk the curry leaf emulsion and drizzle a generous amount over the fish and around the plate. Serve immediately.

Wine Suggestions: Chalone Pinot Noir
Domaine Drouhin Pinot Noir
The sweet seductiveness of the Pinot will complement the delicate flavor of the sole and will stand up to the strength of the emulsion.

Vegetables

Mrs. Ayyer's Vegetable *Biryani* with Tempered Onion-Cucumber *Raita*

Papillote of Spring Vegetables

Tomatoes Stuffed with Potato Korma

Pan-Seared Japanese Eggplant with Feta Cheese

Squash Blossoms with Fennel and Cauliflower Mousse

Spicy Spinach Pancakes

Mung Bean Dumplings with Tomato *Raita*

Fettuccine with White Truffles and Curry Leaves

Mrs. Ayyer's Vegetable *Biryani* with Tempered Onion-Cucumber *Raita*

Serves 6

1 large cucumber

$^1\!/_4$ cup plus 1 tablespoon ghee (see page 15)

$^1\!/_2$ teaspoon mustard seeds

1 cup plain yogurt

1 cup buttermilk

$^1\!/_2$ cup plus 3 tablespoons finely diced onion

Coarse salt, to taste

1 cup $^1\!/_2$-inch dice carrots

1 cup coarsely chopped green beans

2 tablespoons minced fresh cayenne chile

1 tablespoon minced garlic

1 tablespoon minced fresh ginger

3 tablespoons fresh lime juice

1 cup fresh peas

1 teaspoon saffron threads

1 teaspoon ground cumin

$^1\!/_2$ teaspoon Garam Masala (see page 14)

$^1\!/_2$ teaspoon ground turmeric

4 cups cooked basmati rice

$^1\!/_2$ cup toasted cashew nuts, chopped

For years, Mrs. Ayyer was our family cook. When my sister and I were small, Mrs. Ayyer would use just about every trick in her book to get us to eat our meals. Of all of the foods that she would prepare, this is the one dish that I needed absolutely no persuasion to eat. In fact, I would always clean my plate and ask for more. Today, when I make this dish, I am transported back to those innocent years.

1. Peel, seed, and cut the cucumber into $^1\!/_2$-inch dice. Set aside.

2. Heat 1 tablespoon of the ghee in a small sauté pan over medium heat. Add the mustard seeds and sauté for about 3 minutes, or until the seeds begin to pop. Remove immediately from the heat.

3. Combine the yogurt and buttermilk in a mixing bowl. Whisk in the mustard seeds and ghee. Fold in $^1\!/_2$ cup of the onion and the reserved cucumber. Taste and adjust the seasoning with salt. Cover and refrigerate the *raita* until ready to use.

4. Put the carrots and beans in a medium saucepan filled with salted rapidly boiling water and blanch for 30 seconds. Drain well and refresh under cold running water. Pat dry and set aside.

5. Put the remaining $^1\!/_4$ cup of ghee in a large saucepan over medium heat. Add the cayenne chile, garlic, ginger, and the remaining onion and sauté for about 4 minutes, or until golden brown. Add the lime juice. Stir in the peas and the reserved carrots and beans and sauté for 5 minutes. Stir in the saffron,

cumin, garam masala, and turmeric and sauté for 1 minute. Add the rice and continue to sauté for an 5 additional minutes. Stir in the cashews and serve with a bowl of tempered onion-cucumber *raita* on the side.

Wine Suggestions: Zaca Mesa Rousanne
Guigal Côtes du Rhône Blanc
We find that distinctively flavored whites such as these two wines are often the best match for vegetarian dishes.

Papillote of Spring Vegetables

Serves 6

3 tablespoons ghee (see page 15)

1 cup mung bean sprouts

1 cup julienned carrots

1 cup julienned potatoes

1 cup ¼-inch dice zucchini

1 cup tiny cauliflower florets

1 cup ½-inch dice of peeled, cored, and seeded tomatoes

½ teaspoon ajowan

Coarse salt, to taste

¼ cup water

This dish can be prepared with olive oil, so that it is a strictly vegetarian meal. However, I personally prefer the richly aromatic ghee to flavor the vegetables. The *ajowan* adds just the right embellishment to bring out the individual flavors of each vegetable. Although this dish can be served as a main course, it works equally well as an appetizer or side dish.

1. Preheat the oven to 350°F.

2. Cut 6 pieces of parchment paper into 10 x 10-inch squares. Using a pastry brush, lightly coat each sheet with ghee.

3. Combine the sprouts, carrots, potatoes, zucchini, cauliflower, and tomatoes in a mixing bowl. Sprinkle with the *ajowan* and salt. Toss to combine.

4. Place an equal portion of the vegetable mixture into the center of each piece of prepared parchment paper. Lightly sprinkle the vegetables with the water. Pull up the edges of the paper and neatly fold them in and over to create a tightly sealed packet. Place the packets on a baking sheet and bake for 10 minutes. Remove from the oven.

5. Leave the packets sealed, and allow your guests to open them at the table. Serve with warm *nan* or sourdough bread.

Wine Suggestions: Fontana Candida Pinot Grigio
Georges Duboeuf Viognier
Either of these aromatic, distinctive white wines will heighten the simple flavors of this vegetable dish.

Tomatoes Stuffed with Potato Korma

Serves 6

1 tablespoon black cumin seeds

¹/₄ teaspoon cumin seeds

One 2-inch cinnamon stick

6 large ripe tomatoes

6 tablespoons peanut oil

¹/₂ cup finely chopped onions

4 medium potatoes, cooked, peeled, and cut into ¹/₂-inch dice

2 fresh cayenne chiles, stemmed and finely chopped

Coarse salt, to taste

1 cup water

¹/₄ cup half-and-half

¹/₂ cup fresh bread crumbs

¹/₂ cup freshly grated Parmigiano-Reggiano cheese

As I worked on the Vegetables section of this book, I took a nostalgic journey through my memories of childhood. This particular dish became famous in our family when Mrs. Ayyer, our cook, made it as a passed hors d'oeuvre for a party. As the guests lifted the overstuffed vegetables to their mouths, the tomatoes would collapse. My father very politely suggested that perhaps Mrs. Ayyer should consider them for an appetizer to be served at the table. However you serve them, I'm sure you will find them as delicious as we did. (I never thought it possible to improve on Mrs. Ayyer's cooking but my addition of grated Parmesan cheese adds a new slant to her wonderful tomatoes.)

1. Put the black cumin, cumin seeds, and the cinnamon stick in a small sauté pan over medium heat. Cook, stirring frequently, for about 3 minutes, or until the spices are toasted and aromatic. Remove from the heat and cool. Put the spices in a spice grinder and process to a fine powder.

2. Wash the tomatoes and pat dry. Cut out the core and make an opening about 2 inches in diameter around the top of each tomato. Using a teaspoon, scrape out the seeds and membrane. Turn upside down on a double thickness of paper towel to drain.

3. Preheat the oven to 350°F.

4. Heat the oil in a large sauté pan over medium heat. Add the onions and sauté for 3 minutes. Stir in the potatoes, cayenne chiles, the reserved spices, and salt. Add the water and half-

and-half and stir to combine. Lower the heat and cook, stirring frequently, for 10 minutes, adding additional water if necessary to keep the potatoes from getting too dry.

5. Turn the tomatoes upright and, using a tablespoon, fill the cavity of each tomato with the potato mixture. Sprinkle the tops with an equal amount of bread crumbs and cheese. Place the stuffed tomatoes in a shallow baking dish, taking care not to crowd them. Bake for 20 minutes, or until the tomatoes just start to cook and the tops are golden and nicely crusted. Serve immediately.

Wine Suggestions: Ravenswood Vintner's Blend Zinfandel
Tommasi Valpolicella
This highly spiced and extremely flavorful tomato dish calls for a medium-bodied zesty red wine, such as the Zin or the Valpolicella.

Pan-Seared Japanese Eggplant with Feta Cheese

Serves 6

6 large Japanese eggplant
$1/2$ cup peanut oil
Coarse salt, to taste
2 cups crumbled feta cheese
$1/2$ teaspoon ground coriander

Japanese eggplant is extremely quick cooking, simple, and simply delicious! This dish is easy to do and makes a wonderful light lunch, served with a bitter greens and citrus salad, warm bread, and a glass of great wine.

1. Trim each eggplant and cut lengthwise into $1/2$-inch-thick slices. Keep the slices of each eggplant together.
2. Heat half the oil in a large sauté pan over medium heat. In batches, sear the eggplant, adding oil as needed, for about 5 minutes, or just until brown. Season with salt.
3. Fan one complete eggplant out on each of 6 warm dinner plates. Sprinkle the cheese generously over the eggplant and around the plate. Dust each plate with coriander and serve.

Wine Suggestions: J. Vidal Fleury Côtes du Rhône
Saintsbury Cellars Garnet Pinot Noir
A light, fruity red will highlight and balance the complementary flavors of the cheese and the lightly spiced eggplant.

Squash Blossoms
with Fennel and Cauliflower Mousse

Serves 6

1 large fennel bulb

2 cups tiny cauliflower florets

$^1/_2$ cup plus 1 tablespoon ghee (see page 15)

3 tablespoons minced shallots

1 teaspoon crushed fennel seeds

Skin of $^1/_2$ jalapeño chile (see Note)

$^1/_2$ cup heavy cream

Coarse salt, to taste

18 large squash blossoms

I wanted to replicate the texture and flavor of crab mousse–stuffed squash blossoms that I had tasted in France, but I wanted the dish to be vegetarian. Through much experimentation, I found that the combination of cauliflower and fennel fit the bill, making a creamy, delicate mousse. Squash blossoms are usually easy to find during the summer at farmer's markets or roadside vegetable stands. I generally serve these blossoms as a side dish or an appetizer, but with a crisp salad, they would make an excellent main course. When preparing them for an entree, you can easily double the recipe.

1. Trim the fennel, setting aside 6 sprigs of the fronds. Wash the bulb well. Cut the fennel into $^1/_2$-inch dice. Place the fennel and cauliflower in a large saucepan filled with rapidly boiling salted water and blanch for 1 minute. Drain and refresh under cold running water. Pat dry.

2. Heat 3 tablespoons of the ghee in a large sauté pan over medium heat. Add the shallots and sauté for 1 minute. Stir in the fennel and cauliflower, the fennel seeds, and jalapeño skin. Sauté for 5 minutes. Stir in the cream and salt and cook for 1 minute more. Scrape into a blender and puree.

3. Spoon the mousse into a pastry bag fitted with a plain tip. Carefully pipe some mousse into each squash blossom, taking care not to overfill the blossoms, or the mousse will leak out. Twist the ends of the blossoms together to seal them.

4. Heat the remaining 6 tablespoons of ghee in a large nonstick

sauté pan over medium heat. Add the squash blossoms, a few at a time, and sauté for about 3 minutes, or just until the blossoms soften.

5. Place 3 squash blossoms on each of 6 warm plates. Pipe a bit of the remaining mousse at the end of each blossom and garnish with a fennel frond.

Note: Wearing rubber gloves, use a vegetable peeler with a swivel blade to peel off a thin layer of skin from the jalapeño.

Wine Suggestions: Beringer Fumé Blanc
Sterling Sauvignon Blanc
The herbaceousness of the Sauvignon accents this dish to its fullest.

Spicy Spinach Pancakes

Serves 6

3 cups split black lentils

2 quarts plus 1 cup cold water

1 cup buttermilk

$1/2$ cup cooked rice

$1/4$ cup rice flour

1 teaspoon coarsely ground black
   pepper

1 cup finely chopped fresh spinach

$1/4$ cup peanut oil

Cumin-Scented Tomato Coulis
   (optional, see page 34)

This is a another delicious recipe from my childhood. These pancakes make a very nutritious luncheon dish as well as a wonderful base for many meat dishes. If you don't want to make the coulis, just drizzle a bit of warm ghee over the top.

1. Put the black lentils in a large mixing bowl. Add the water and allow to soak for 4 hours. Drain, reserving the soaking water.
2. Put the lentils in a blender and process, adding soaking water as necessary to make a soupy puree. Add the buttermilk, cooked rice, rice flour, and pepper and process to a pancakelike batter. Add the spinach and process just to blend.
3. Heat 1 tablespoon of the oil in a nonstick griddle over medium heat. Slowly pour in 2 ounces of batter to make a round pancake. Cook for about 1 minute, or until the batter is set and the bottom is golden. Turn and cook the other side until golden. Continue making pancakes until you have used all the batter.
4. Serve 3 pancakes per person with the coulis spooned over the top, if desired.

Wine Suggestions: Veramonte Primus
Santa Carolina Reserve Merlot
A soft, spicy Merlot perfectly balances the straightforward flavors of this pancake dish.

Mung Bean Dumplings with Tomato *Raita*

Serves 6

3 cups split mung beans

1 quart cold water

2 tablespoons curry leaf chiffonade

1 cup plain yogurt

1 cup buttermilk

$\frac{1}{2}$ cup cored, peeled, seeded, and
finely chopped tomatoes

$\frac{1}{4}$ cup finely chopped onions

$\frac{1}{2}$ teaspoon minced jalapeño chile

Coarse salt, to taste

2 fresh cayenne chiles, minced

1 teaspoon crushed cumin seeds

4 cups peanut oil

This is another simple and easy recipe that is based on a traditional Indian afternoon snack. The mung bean puree and the *raita* can be made early in the day. If you wish, you can even fry the dumplings, drain them well, and reheat them in the oven just before serving. This dumpling-and-*raita* combination works well as an hors d'oeuvre (make the dumplings very small and use the *raita* as a dip) or as an appetizer.

1. Put the mung beans in the water and allow them to soak for at least 4 hours.

2. Working with about 6 leaves at a time, stack the curry leaves, one on top of the other, and roll them up, cigar fashion. Cut each roll, crosswise, into $\frac{1}{4}$-inch pieces. (These ragged strips are called a chiffonade.)

3. Whisk together the yogurt and buttermilk in a mixing bowl. Stir in the tomatoes, onions, curry leaves, jalapeño, and salt. Cover and refrigerate the *raita* until ready to use.

4. Drain the mung beans, reserving the soaking water. Put the mung beans in a blender and, adding the soaking water as necessary, process to a very smooth and thick puree. (The puree has to be thick enough to hold together when it is deep-fried.) Pour the puree into a mixing bowl. Stir in the cayenne chiles, cumin seeds, and salt to taste.

5. Heat the oil in a deep-fat fryer to 365°F on a candy thermometer. Drop the mung bean batter by the tablespoonful into the hot oil, taking care not to crowd the pan. Fry, turning

as necessary, for about 3 minutes, or until the dumplings are cooked through and golden brown. Using a slotted spoon, transfer the dumplings to a double thickness of paper towel to drain. Continue frying until all of the batter has been used. Serve hot with a bowl of tomato *raita* on the side.

Wine Suggestions: Fortant de France Syrah
P. Antinori Santa Cristina
A medium-dry, sturdy red wine will enhance the lightly spiced yet simple combination of flavors in this dish.

Fettuccine with White Truffles and Curry Leaves

Serves 6

½ cup fresh curry leaves
2 cloves garlic, minced
1 ½ pounds fresh fettuccine
¼ cup extra virgin olive oil
Sea salt, to taste
2 tablespoons (about 1 ounce) fresh
    white truffle shavings

I was, once upon a birthday, given a bottle of Domaine de la Romanée-Conti le Montrachet 1992. I longed to enjoy it with something very special, yet simple, so I created this dish. It was an absolutely heavenly meal, with the truffles complementing but not competing with the wine.

1. Remove the curry leaves from the refrigerator at least 1 hour before you are going to use them. This will allow them to release their bouquet more quickly when added to the pasta.
2. Put the garlic in a small saucepan filled with rapidly boiling water and blanch for 30 seconds. Drain well.
3. Place the fettuccine in a large pot filled with rapidly boiling salted water and cook for about 4 minutes, or until *al dente*. Drain well.
4. Heat the oil in a large nonstick sauté pan over medium heat. Add the garlic and then the fettuccine and toss to combine. Add the salt. Toss the truffle shavings into the fettuccine, and then add the curry leaves. Toss to combine and serve immediately in warm pasta bowls.

Wine Suggestions: Drouhin Puligny-Montrachet
Domaine Laroche Chablis Premier Cru
The earthiness of a white burgundy is a perfect complement for the earthy perfume of the white truffles.

Desserts

Power Chocolate Soufflé

Anise-Flavored Chocolate Meringues with Dark
  Chocolate Sauce

Pepper-Spiced Figs in Red Wine

Spiced Apple Tarts

Fresh Fruit with Herb-Infused Syrup

Pan-Seared Peaches with Brown Butter and
  Jaggery

Lemongrass Sorbet with Sweet Spice Madeleines

Frozen Ginger-Peach Soufflés

Coconut Rice Pudding

Cardamom Crème Brûlée

Chilled Mango-Saffron Soup

*We have not offered wine pairings with every dessert because many desserts are best when eaten alone
in their sugary goodness. In these instances, you might want to follow the dessert with any number of
marvelous after-dinner liqueurs or brandies.*

Power Chocolate Soufflé

Serves 6

6 large egg whites, at room
 temperature
1/2 teaspoon cream of tartar
10 ounces bittersweet chocolate,
 melted

This is an all-time restaurant favorite! Although it is put together at the last minute, which may seem daunting, this soufflé is so simple that I suggest that you perfect it as an always-on-hand fancy dessert. Just before dinner, beat the egg whites and melt the chocolate. Refrigerate the egg whites until ready to use, and keep the melted chocolate over warm, but not hot, water. At dessert time, you can put the soufflés together, 1–2–3! By the time the table is cleared and the coffee is made, the soufflés will be out of the oven and ready to eat.

1. Preheat the oven to 350°F.
2. Place the egg whites and cream of tartar in the bowl of a electric mixer fitted with a whip. Beat the egg whites until medium-firm peaks form. Using a spatula, gently fold the melted chocolate into the egg whites.
3. Place an equal portion of the soufflé mixture into each of six 6-ounce soufflé dishes or into one 2-quart soufflé dish. Place the filled dishes into a baking dish large enough to hold them without the insides touching. Add hot water to come halfway up the sides of the soufflé dishes. Bake for about 5 minutes, or until the soufflés have risen, and the edges have taken on some color.
4. Remove the soufflés from the oven. Carefully lift the dishes from the hot water and wipe the bottoms dry. Place each one on a heat-proof dessert plate and serve immediately.

Note: For an over-the-top experience, serve some warm bittersweet chocolate sauce with the soufflés. Beat together until well blended 8 ounces chopped bittersweet chocolate, $^1/_3$ cup heavy cream, and 4 tablespoons ($^1/_2$ stick) unsalted butter in the top of a double boiler. When serving individual soufflés, use a soup spoon to open the centers as you serve them and pour a few tablespoons of the warm chocolate sauce into the soufflés. When serving from one large soufflé, drizzle the warm sauce over each portion.

Wine Suggestions: Taylor LBV Port
Dow's Tawny Port
A sturdy port is always a wonderful counterbalance for a chocolate dessert.

Anise-Flavored Chocolate Meringues with Dark Chocolate Sauce

Serves 6

4 large egg whites at room temperature

$1/2$ teaspoon chocolate extract

$1/4$ teaspoon anise extract

$1/2$ cup superfine sugar

1 teaspoon toasted anise seed

6 ounces bittersweet chocolate

$1/4$ cup espresso or other strong coffee

2 tablespoons anisette

$1/2$ pound (2 sticks) unsalted butter, softened

Pinch of salt

$1/2$ cup chocolate-covered coffee beans (approximately, see Note)

Too much of a good thing? Not if you like chocolate! I often put a pinch of cayenne into the meringues—try it, you'll find that it heightens the chocolate flavor. By the way, this chocolate sauce is so thick and rich that when it has cooled, you can use it to frost a cake.

1. Preheat the oven to its lowest setting.

2. Put the egg whites and the chocolate and anise extracts in the large bowl of an electric mixer and beat, at high speed, until the egg whites hold a firm peak. Gradually beat in the sugar and continue beating until the egg whites are quite stiff and very shiny. Fold in the anise seed.

3. Line a baking sheet with parchment paper. Spoon the meringue mixture into a pastry bag filled with a large fluted tip. Pipe eight 3-inch circles onto the baking sheet to form the bases. Then pipe a border around each circle to form a little bowl. (I make 8 meringues to allow for the inevitable breakage.)

4. Bake for about $2^{1}/2$ hours, or until they are crisp, very dry, and slightly colored. You do not want them to brown. Allow to cool on wire racks. Store in an airtight container until ready to use. (Meringues quickly take on moisture, so keep them dry and crisp.)

5. While the meringues are baking, place the chocolate, coffee, and anisette in a small heavy saucepan over medium heat. Cook, stirring constantly, for about 3 minutes or until the chocolate has melted; keep the heat very low so the chocolate

doesn't burn. Remove from the heat and beat in the butter, a bit at a time, and the salt. If the mixture cools down too much to absorb the butter, return it to very low heat, but do not stir in the butter while it is on the heat.

6. Place a meringue in the center of each of 6 warm dessert plates. Fill the center of each meringue with the chocolate sauce and drizzle the plate with a bit more. Scatter chocolate-covered coffee beans around the plate and serve.

Note: When purchasing chocolate-covered coffee beans, make sure you get real beans. I have often been fooled by candies that look exactly like coffee beans but are, in fact, just chocolate.

Pepper-Spiced Figs in Red Wine

Serves 6

4 cups red wine
3/4 cup jaggery (see page 18)
2 tablespoons balsamic vinegar
1/2 vanilla bean, split
1 2-inch piece lemongrass, chopped
1 very small dried red chile
1 tablespoon black peppercorns
18 dried black figs
1 cup crème fraîche
6 small sprigs fresh mint

This spicy-sweet wine and fruit combination is, to me, the perfect ending to almost any meal. I have based it on the classic French technique of poaching fresh fruit in either red or white wine but have added some Indian spice to make it my own.

1. Combine the red wine and jaggery in a large saucepan over medium heat. Cook, stirring frequently, for about 5 minutes, or until the jaggery has dissolved. Stir in the vinegar, vanilla bean, lemongrass, chile, and peppercorns. Bring to a boil. Add the figs, and bring to a boil again. Lower the heat and simmer for about 25 minutes, or until the figs are soft and the liquid has reduced to about 1 1/2 cups. (If necessary, remove the figs when they are done and continue reducing the liquid.)

2. Cut the figs in half and set aside.

3. Strain the sauce through a fine strainer. Pour an equal portion of the warm sauce into each of 6 shallow soup bowls. Place 6 fig halves on the sauce and add a dollop of crème fraîche to the center. Nestle a mint sprig into the crème fraîche and serve.

Variations: Replace the dried figs with fresh ones. Reduce the wine mixture and, while it is still hot, add the fresh figs and allow them to marinate in the reduced syrup for about 5 minutes, so that they warm slightly and perfume the liquid. If you don't have crème fraîche, use fine quality frozen yogurt or ice cream.

Spiced Apple Tarts

Serves 6

6 medium tart apples

$^1/_4$ cup light brown sugar

1 teaspoon ground cinnamon

$^1/_4$ teaspoon ground mace

$^1/_4$ teaspoon ground ginger

Pinch of ground cayenne

1 teaspoon grated lemon zest

1 tablespoon Wondra flour (see Note)

12 tablespoons (1 $^1/_2$ sticks) unsalted
   butter, melted

6 sheets phyllo dough

3 tablespoons confectioners' sugar,
   plus an optional 3 tablespoons for
   sprinkling

$^1/_2$ cup heavy cream, whipped, or 1
   pint vanilla ice cream (optional)

This is my very best version of every American mom's apple pie. Phyllo dough is a lifesaver for someone like me, who was not raised with traditional tarts and pies and therefore has very little interest in or skill at making them. The recipe produces a crisp, tasty crust for these slightly spicy apples.

1. Line a baking sheet with parchment paper.

2. Preheat the oven to 375°F.

3. Peel, core, quarter, and cut the apples into very thin slices. Place them in a mixing bowl. Sprinkle with the brown sugar, cinnamon, mace, ginger, and cayenne. Toss in the lemon zest and flour. Drizzle $^1/_4$ cup of the butter over the top and gently toss to coat.

4. Cover the phyllo sheets with a damp kitchen towel to keep them from drying out. Working with 1 sheet at a time and using a pastry brush, brush a phyllo sheet with melted butter. Fold the sheet in half and brush with butter again. Repeat this step one more time. Using a pastry cutter, carefully cut a 5-inch circle from the folded phyllo. Set the circle aside, covered with a damp towel to keep the dough moist. Using the remaining phyllo sheets and butter, make 5 more circles as described above.

5. Working with 1 phyllo circle at a time, beginning with the outside edge, arrange slightly overlapping circles of apple slices to completely cover the dough. The center will be slightly higher than the outside edge because of the overlap. Continue working until you have 6 apple-covered circles.

6. Place the tarts on the prepared baking sheet. Bake for 18 minutes, or until the apples are tender and have taken on some color.

7. Raise the oven heat to broil.

8. With the tarts still on it, carefully lift the parchment paper from the baking sheet and set it on a flat surface. Sprinkle 3 tablespoons of the confectioners' sugar over the hot tarts. Using a spatula, lift the tarts from the parchment and place them back onto the baking sheet. Broil the tarts for 3 minutes, or until the apple edges are nicely browned. Remove from the broiler and place them on a wire rack to cool.

9. Serve warm or at room temperature, sprinkled with additional confectioners' sugar or with whipped or ice cream on the side, if desired.

Note: Wondra flour is an extremely fine-grained flour available in supermarkets.

Wine Suggestions: Nonalcoholic Sparkling Apple Cider
Calvados

Fresh Fruit with Herb-Infused Syrup

Serves 6

3 ¹/₂ cups Sauternes wine

2 cups water

¹/₂ cup sugar

1 teaspoon minced fresh ginger

¹/₄ teaspoon ground cardamom

6 sprigs fresh rosemary

6 medium very ripe fresh peaches or
    nectarines, peeled, or 12 large fresh
    apricots, peeled

6 small sprigs fresh mint

1 cup crumbled amaretti cookies

This should be made only when summer fruits are at their ripest and most succulent. However, the lightly spiced syrup is so delicious that, in the winter, you might want to poach dried fruit in the syrup as it reduces. It won't be as delicate, but it will be delicious.

1. Combine the wine, water, sugar, ginger, cardamom, and rosemary in a medium heavy-bottomed saucepan over medium-high heat. Bring to a boil. Lower the heat and simmer for about 30 minutes, or until the liquid has reduced by one half. Remove from the heat and strain through a fine sieve, discarding the solids.

2. Put the fruit in a nonreactive container. Pour the hot syrup over the fruit and allow it to marinate for at least 2 hours at room temperature. Cover and refrigerate until ready to serve.

3. Pour an equal portion of the syrup into each of 6 shallow bowls. Place a peach or nectarine or 2 apricots into each bowl, stem side up. Place a mint sprig into the stem end. Sprinkle with crumbled amaretti cookies and serve.

Wine Suggestions: Bonny Doon Muscat
Coppo Moscato d'Asti
The delicate natural sweetness of the Muscat will complement the sweetness of the fresh fruit.

Pan-Seared Peaches
with Brown Butter and Jaggery

Serves 6

12 firm but ripe small peaches,
    preferably freestone (see Note)
Pinch of salt
Pinch of freshly ground black pepper
$^1/_2$ cup ghee (see page 15)
$^1/_2$ cup jaggery (see page 18)
2 tablespoons sherry or port wine
    (optional)

This simple dessert is best served when peaches are at their ripest. I use sherry to fortify the syrup, but it is not absolutely necessary. For an additional treat, serve some Sweet Spice Madeleines (see page 198) with the warm fruit.

1. Wash the peaches and pat dry. Cut in half lengthwise, remove the pits, and season the cut sides with salt and pepper. (This will set the enzymes and heighten the flavor.) Place the peaches, cut sides down, on a platter or other nonreactive surface, and allow to rest for 30 minutes.

2. Heat the ghee in a large sauté pan over medium heat. Add the peaches, cut sides down, and cook for about 3 minutes, or until the fruit and ghee begin to brown. Add the jaggery. Cook for about 5 minutes, or until the peaches begin to soften and the ghee and jaggery mixture is golden and syrupy. Add the sherry and cook for an additional minute.

3. Place 4 peach halves, cut sides down, in each of 6 shallow dessert bowls or soup plates. Pour syrup over each portion and serve.

Note: Plums, apricots, or nectarines can be used in place of the peaches.

Wine Suggestions: Château Rieussac Sauternes
Château de Malle Sauternes
The lusciousness of a beautiful Sauternes will heighten the rich fresh flavor of this dish.

Lemongrass Sorbet
with Sweet Spice Madeleines

Serves 6

1 cup water
1 cup sugar
1 cup chopped lemongrass
2 cups fresh lemon juice
¼ cup minced fresh cilantro
Sweet Spice Madeleines (recipe
   follows)

The lemongrass adds a subtle hint of Asia, while the cilantro adds a wallop! This refreshing sorbet is made even more special with the addition of the lovely little madeleines at the side of the bowl. My Proustian journey takes me to the aromas of my Eastern childhood, when the deliciously fragrant smells of sweet cardamom, cinnamon, and cloves filled our house. These delicate cookies can be served with almost any dessert in this book or alone, with a cup of herbal tea.

1. Combine the water, sugar, and lemongrass in a small saucepan over high heat. Cook, stirring constantly, for about 4 minutes, or until the sugar has dissolved. Remove from the heat and allow to cool to room temperature. Strain through a fine sieve.
2. Combine the lemon juice and cilantro with the lemongrass-infused syrup. Pour into an ice cream freezer and freeze according to the manufacturer's instructions.
3. When the sorbet is ready, place a scoop into each of 6 well-chilled, small glass bowls. Place 2 madeleines at opposite sides of each bowl and serve.

1. Preheat the oven to 450°F.

2. Spray two 12-cup madeleine tins with vegetable-oil spray. Set aside.

3. In a medium bowl, sift together the flour, cardamom, cinnamon, and cloves. Set aside.

4. Combine the eggs, sugar, and zest in a large heat-proof mixing bowl. Place the bowl over a pan of very hot water, without allowing the bottom to touch the heat. Whisk occasionally until the mixture is warm. Using a hand-held electric mixer, beat the egg mixture at high speed until it is extremely light and fluffy and has tripled in volume. Stir in the vanilla.

5. Gently fold in the flour mixture and then the ghee, taking care not to beat them into the batter.

6. Carefully scoop the batter into the prepared tins, filling the molds about two thirds full. Bake for about 10 minutes, or until golden. Remove from the molds and allow to cool on a wire rack.

7. Store the madeleines, tightly covered, for up to 3 days.

Sweet Spice Madeleines
Makes about 2 dozen

2 cups all-purpose flour
$1/2$ teaspoon ground cardamom
$1/2$ teaspoon ground cinnamon
$1/4$ teaspoon ground cloves
4 large eggs
$1 1/2$ cups superfine sugar
$1/2$ teaspoon finely grated lemon zest
1 teaspoon pure vanilla extract
$1 1/2$ cups ghee (see page 15)

Frozen Ginger-Peach Soufflés

1 ½ pounds very ripe peaches
1 teaspoon fresh ginger juice (see page 12)
1 cup granulated sugar
6 large egg yolks
½ cup white corn syrup
¼ cup nonfat vanilla yogurt
1 ½ cups heavy cream
1 teaspoon pure vanilla extract
1 tablespoon confectioners' sugar
6 fresh blueberries
6 very small sprigs fresh mint

For the home cook, a frozen soufflé is a dream come true. It can be made ahead of time, frozen for up to one week, and then presented as a spectacular finish to a meal. Feel free to substitute any ripe, soft, low-acid fruit for the peaches.

1. Put the peaches in a pan filled with rapidly boiling water for about 30 seconds, or until their skins just begin to loosen. Using a slotted spoon, immediately remove the peaches from the water and slip off the skins. Coarsely chop the peaches, put them in a saucepan, and stir in the ginger juice. Add ½ cup of the granulated sugar and stir to combine. Place over medium-high heat and bring to a simmer. Lower the heat and simmer for about 5 minutes, or until the peaches are very soft. Remove from the heat and allow to cool.

2. Meanwhile, prepare the soufflé dishes. Cut six 14 x 7-inch strips of aluminum foil. Fold the strips in half lengthwise and wrap 1 strip around each of six 6-ounce soufflé dishes to come up about ¾ inch above the rim of the dish. Fold the ends of each strip together and pinch to close firmly. Or alternatively, prepare a 1 ½ quart-soufflé dish in the same fashion. Set aside.

3. Combine the egg yolks, corn syrup, and ¼ cup of the granulated sugar in the top half of a double boiler set over gently simmering water. Do not allow the water to touch the bottom of the top pan. Heat the egg mixture, whisking

constantly, for about 5 minutes, or until a candy thermometer inserted into mixture reads 170°F. Immediately whisk in the yogurt and remove the top half of the double boiler from the heat. Scrape the egg mixture into a mixing bowl and, using an electric mixer, beat until very thick and cool to the touch. Set aside.

4. Combine the heavy cream and vanilla with the remaining sugar in the bowl of an electric mixer. Beat for about 4 minutes, or until soft peaks form. Gently fold the egg yolk mixture into the whipped cream. When well blended, fold in the peach mixture. When well incorporated, spoon the soufflé mixture into the prepared dishes, allowing

the mixture to come to the top of the foil wraps. Using a spatula, smooth the tops and cover with plastic film. Place in the freezer for at least 8 hours, or until frozen solid.

5. When ready to serve, remove the soufflés from the freezer. Carefully remove and discard the foil wraps. Place a soufflé in the center of each of 6 dessert plates. Place the confectioners' sugar in a small fine sieve and gently shake it over each plate. Place a blueberry in the center of each soufflé and tuck a mint sprig into it. Or if you are serving a large soufflé, scoop the soufflé into ice cream dishes or wine goblets and garnish as described above. Serve immediately.

Wine Suggestions: Michel Picard Vouvray
Martini & Rossi Asti Spumante

Coconut Rice Pudding

Serves 6

⅓ cup basmati rice, well washed

5 cups milk

1 cup coconut milk (see page 18)

½ cup sugar

½ teaspoon ground cardamom

Pinch of saffron threads

1 cup chopped pistachios

2 tablespoons grated fresh coconut

¼ teaspoon screw pine essence (see
  Note)

This is probably the only dessert that I serve in the restaurant that might, in one version or another, have been served in my home in India. I find that everyone loves rice pudding, even my rather exotic rendition.

1. Combine the rice with 2 cups of the milk and the coconut milk in a large heavy-bottomed saucepan over medium-high heat. Bring to a boil. Lower the heat and cook, stirring frequently, for about 30 minutes, or until all of the milk has been absorbed by the rice. Do not allow the rice to stick or burn.

2. Add the remaining milk, the sugar, cardamom, and saffron and continue to cook, stirring frequently, for about 1 hour, or until the pudding is very thick.

3. Stir in 1/2 cup of the chopped pistachios along with the coconut and screw pine essence and cook for an additional 5 minutes.

4. Remove from the heat and allow to cool slightly. Pour into dessert bowls, cover with plastic film, and refrigerate for at least 2 hours, or until well chilled.

5. Serve chilled, garnished with the remaining pistachios.

Note: Screw pine essence is available in East Indian markets.

Cardamom Crème Brûlée

Serves 6

12 large egg yolks, beaten
1 cup granulated sugar
4 cups heavy cream
1 teaspoon freshly ground cardamom
   (see Note)
1 cup light brown sugar

Just a few short years ago, crème brûlée was found only in four-star French restaurants. Now almost everybody makes one using a favorite and often exotic flavoring. This ice-cold custard with the crackling sugar top is the most popular dessert at my restaurant. So much so that I sometimes think it is the only dessert I should make. Perhaps it is the ease of preparation that makes me think so!

1. Preheat the oven to 325°F.
2. In a large heat-proof mixing bowl, whisk together the egg yolks and sugar.
3. Place the cream in a heavy bottomed saucepan over medium heat. Warm just until little bubbles form around the edge. Remove from the heat and, whisking constantly, pour into the egg and sugar mixture. Add the cardamom and continue whisking until the sugar has dissolved and the mixture is well combined.
4. Pour the mixture through a very fine sieve into 6 crème brûlée dishes, filling them only half full. Place the dishes into a shallow baking dish large enough to hold them without crowding. Place the dish on the middle rack of oven. Working quickly to preserve the heat, finish filling the dishes with the custard mixture, making sure that it comes right to the top of each dish. Then carefully fill the baking dish with very hot tap water so it comes halfway up the sides of the filled dishes. Bake for about 25 minutes, or until the custard is set in the center.

5. Remove the custards to a wire rack to cool. Refrigerate for at least 3 hours, or until ready to use.

6. When ready to serve, preheat the broiler.

7. Pass the brown sugar through a fine sieve to eliminate all lumps. Generously sprinkle the top of each chilled custard with an equal portion of the brown sugar, taking care to cover all of the custard, so that it gives an even finish. Place the chilled crème brûlée dishes under the preheated broiler and broil for about 2 minutes, or until the tops are crackling brown. Remove from the broiler and serve immediately.

Note: When I make this dish, I often grind the cardamom in a coffee grinder so that it picks up just a hint of coffee (in my kitchen, usually espresso) flavor.

Wine Suggestion: Royal Tokaji Red
This quite sweet but well-balanced Tokaji is a stunning companion to this lightly spiced and very rich dessert.

Chilled Mango-Saffron Soup

7 large, very ripe mangoes

1 cup fresh orange juice

$\frac{1}{2}$ cup Muscat de Venise or another
    sweet wine

$\frac{1}{4}$ teaspoon saffron threads

Pinch of ground cardamom

1 to 2 tablespoons sugar
    (approximately)

1 tablespoon fresh lime juice

2 tablespoons chopped fresh mint

Fruit soups as desserts are rather new to me but I find them so addictive in their freshness that I now make them often—especially since they are easy to prepare ahead to have on hand for a busy night. Although this soup is best made with very ripe fresh mangoes, you can also make it with canned sweet Indian mangoes. If you need to thin the soup, try seltzer. It adds a bit of sparkle.

1. Peel and seed 6 of the mangoes. Place the pulp in a blender along with the orange juice, wine, saffron, and cardamom. Process until very smooth. If the soup is too thick, add seltzer or water, a bit at a time, to thin it. Taste and adjust the flavor with sugar and lime juice. Pour into a nonreactive container. Cover and refrigerate for at least 3 hours, or until well chilled.

2. Peel and cut the remaining mango into $\frac{1}{4}$-inch dice. Set aside.

3. When ready to serve, pour equal portions of the soup into each of 6 chilled shallow soup bowls. Fold some diced mango into each bowl. Sprinkle the top with mint and serve.

Sources

SPICES, CONDIMENTS, ASIAN PRODUCTS
Adriana's Caravan
404 Vanderbilt Street
Brooklyn, New York 11218
(800) 316-0820
www.adriana'scaravan.com

The Oriental Pantry
423 Great Road
Acton, Mass. 01720
(800) 828-0368
www.orientalpantry.com

Penzey's Spice House
P.O. Box 14348
Waukesha, Wisconsin 53187
(414) 574-0278
www.penzeys.com

Kalustyan Orient Export Trading Corp
123 Lexington Avenue
New York, NY 10016
(212) 685-3451

Sultan's Delight
P.O Box 090302
Brooklyn , NY 11209
(718)745-6844

FISH AND SHELLFISH
Browne Trading Corporation
260 Commercial Street
Portland, ME 04101
(800)944-9848
www.brown-trading.com

FOIE GRAS AND GAME AND SPECIALTY MEATS
D'Artagnan
399-419 Saint Paul Avenue
Jersey City, New Jersey 07306
(800) DAR-TAGN or (201) 792-0748

SPECIALTY FOODS, CHEESE GOURMET GROCERIES
Dean & Deluca
560 Broadway
New York, New York 10012
(800) 221-7714
www.dean-deluca.com

Zabar's
2245 Broadway
New York, New York 10024
(212) 787-2000

SPECIALTY KITCHENWARE AND APPLIANCES
Bridge Kitchenware
214 East 52nd Street
New York, NY 10022
(212) 688-4220
fax: (212)758-5387

Index

couscous, Israeli, poussins smoked on sandalwood
chips with, 120–21
crab:
    crustillant with raspberry sauce, 36–37
    purses with cumin-scented tomato coulis,
        34–35
    soft-shell, with cashew crust and carrot-ginger
        chutney, 30–32
    soup with sweet spices and ginger juice,
        50–51
cranberry coulis, buffalo rib-eye with black pepper
    and coriander crust with, 95–96
crème brûlée, cardamom, 204–6
crisp purses with shrimp, scallops, and mint-ginger
    sauce, 38–39
crostini of salmon with lemon-leek sauce,
    70–71
cucumber:
    -onion *raita*, tempered, Mrs. Ayyer's vegetable
        biryani with, 170–71
    soup with dill and mustard seeds, chilled,
        58–59
cumin, 10
    red snapper with garlic, purple potatoes and,
        163–65
    -scented tomato coulis, 34–35
    -scented tomatoes, vegetable purses with,
        45–47
    seeds, black, 9
curry, curried:
    blackberry sauce, baby lamb racks with curry
        leaf–black pepper crust and, 103–5
    blueberry sauce, tenderloin of pork with black
        mustard rub, collard greens and, 88–89
    butternut squash soup, velouté of, 60
    masala, Madras, fillet of sea bass with, 161–62
    sauce, caramelized, duck breasts with confit of
        sweet potatoes and, 129–30
    spice blend, 14
curry leaf(ves):
    –black pepper crust, baby lamb racks with
        curried blackberry sauce and, 103–5
    emulsion, Dover sole with, 166–67
    fettuccine with white truffles and, 183

Indian, broccoli and green pea soup with
    mustard seeds and, 54

dal blinis, sevruga caviar with, 26–27
desserts, 184–207
    anise-flavored chocolate meringues with dark
        chocolate sauce, 188–90
    cardamom crème brûlée, 204–6
    chilled mango-saffron soup, 207
    coconut rice pudding, 202
    fresh fruit with herb-infused syrup, 195
    frozen ginger-peach soufflés, 200–201
    lemongrass sorbet with sweet spice madeleines,
        198–99
    pan-seared peaches with brown butter and
        jaggery, 196
    pepper-spiced figs in red wine, 191
    power chocolate soufflé, 186–87
    spiced apple tarts, 192–94
dhana dal, in antelope chops with blackberry-ginger
    chutney, 135–37
dill:
    chilled cucumber soup with mustard seeds and,
        58–59
    and turmeric emulsion, fillet of salmon with,
        144–45
Dover sole with curry leaf emulsion, 166–67
duck breasts with caramelized curry sauce and
    confit of sweet potatoes, 129–30
dumplings, mung bean, with tomato *raita*, 181–82

eggplant, pan-seared Japanese, with feta cheese, 177
essences, infusing of, 18

fats and oils, 15–16
fava bean puree seasoned with hot spices, 80
fennel and cauliflower mousse, squash blossoms
    with, 178–79
fennel seeds, 10
    foie gras with gratin of ginger, spring asparagus
        and, 40–42

fennel seeds (*cont.*):

    -ginger vinaigrette, golden trout with, 140–41

fenugreek seeds, 12

feta cheese, pan-seared Japanese eggplant with, 177

fettuccine with white truffles and curry leaves, 183

figs, pepper-spiced, in red wine, 191

fillet:

    of beef with butternut squash consommé,
        93–94

    of salmon with dill and turmeric emulsion,
        144–45

    of sea bass with Madras curry masala, 161–62

firing up a recipe, 19

fish, 138–67

    marinating of, 18

    see also specific fish

foie gras:

    with fennel seeds, gratin of ginger, and spring
        asparagus, 40–42

    with French lentils and truffle confit, 43–44

fresh fruit with herb-infused syrup, 195

fried leek nests, 148–50

frozen ginger-peach soufflés, 200–201

fruit:

    fresh, with herb-infused syrup, 195

    spiced basmati rice with pine nuts and, 84–85

    see also specific fruits

game, 122–37

    see also specific game

garam masala, 14

garlic:

    parcels of chicken with amaranth and, 110–11

    potato gratin with onions, saffron and, 83

    red snapper with cumin, purple potatoes and, 163–65

    -scented zucchini, pan-seared scallops with, 72–73

ghee, 15

ginger, 12

    -blackberry chutney, antelope chops with, 135–37

    -carrot chutney, soft-shell crab with cashew
    crust and, 30–32

    chicken with coconut milk, lemongrass and, 119

    -fennel vinaigrette, golden trout with, 140–41

gratin of, foie gras with fennel seeds, spring
    asparagus and, 40–42

juice, crab soup with sweet spices and, 50–51

-mint sauce, crisp purses with shrimp, scallops
    and, 38–39

-peach soufflés, frozen, 200–201

-tamarind chutney, swordfish rubbed with,
    148–50

golden trout with ginger-fennel vinaigrette,
    140–41

gratin:

    of ginger, foie gras with fennel seeds, spring
        asparagus and, 40–42

    potato, with onions, garlic, and saffron, 83

    savory spinach, 78–79

greens, baby, carpaccio of cured beef with mung
    bean polenta and, 64–66

grits, Indian, venison racks with sun-dried tomato
    chutney and, 133–34

grouper with mango-jalapeño sauce, 153–54

halibut with lime-leek beurre blanc and cauliflower
    bouquets, 158–60

herbes de Provence, see Provençal herb(s)

herb-infused syrup, fresh fruit with, 195

honey-tandoori emulsion, oven-roasted quail with
    quinoa with almond sprouts, baby bok choy and,
    127–28

hors d'oeuvres and appetizers, 24–27

    crab crustillant with raspberry sauce, 36–37

    crab purses with cumin-scented tomato coulis,
        34–35

    crisp purses with shrimp, scallops, and mint-
        ginger sauce, 38–39

    foie gras with fennel seeds, gratin of ginger, and
        spring asparagus, 40–42

    foie gras with French lentils and truffle confit,
        43–44

    lemon-cilantro ceviche of scallops, 33

    roulade of tuna tartare with unfiltered sesame
        oil and brunois of green mango, 28–29

    sevruga caviar with dal blinis, 26–27

    soft-shell crab with cashew crust and carrot-

ginger chutney, 30–32
vegetable purses with cumin-scented tomatoes,
45–46
Hyderabad *biryani*, tea-smoked quail with, 124–26

Indian spiced ratatouille, 81–82
infused oils, 16
infusing essences, 18

jaggery, 18
pan-seared peaches with brown butter and, 196–97
jalapeño-mango sauce, grouper with, 153–54

kalonji, 9
korma, potato, tomatoes stuffed with, 174–76

lamb:
racks, baby, with curry leaf–
black pepper crust and curried blackberry
sauce, 103–5
roasted leg of, with mint chutney and mint-
flavored potatoes, 101–2
stew with vindaloo spices and sweet squash and
turnips, 106–7
leek:
-lemon sauce, crostini of salmon with, 70–71
-lime beurre blanc, halibut with cauliflower
bouquets and, 158–60
nests, fried, 148–50
lemon:
-cilantro ceviche of scallops, 33
-leek sauce, crostini of salmon with, 70–71
lemongrass:
chicken with coconut milk, ginger and, 119
sorbet with sweet spice madeleines, 198–99
lentil(s):
French, foie gras with truffle confit and, 43–44
ragout, Cornish game hens with spicy, 116–18
tempered, cassoulet of veal with Provençal herbs
and, 97–98

lime:
-leek beurre blanc, halibut with cauliflower
bouquets and, 158–60
-scented spring vegetables, oven-roasted chicken
with, 112–13
lobster:
coconut milk soup with toasted poppy seeds
and, 55
tail with red and yellow pepper coulis and
potato roulade, 67–69
lotus leaf, veal medallions wrapped in, 98–100

mace, 12
madeleines, sweet spice, lemongrass sorbet with,
198–99
Madras curry masala, fillet of sea bass with, 161–62
mango:
green, roulade of tuna tartare with unfiltered
sesame oil and brunois of, 28–29
-jalapeño sauce, grouper with, 153–54
-papaya salsa, opakapaka with, 151–52
pickle, Indian, in South Indian barbecue with
collard greens and black-eyed peas, 90–92
-saffron soup, chilled, 207
marinating meats or fish, 14
masala, Madras curry, fillet of sea bass with,
161–62
meat, 86–107
marinating of, 18
see also specific meats
meringues, anise-flavored chocolate, with dark
chocolate sauce, 188–90
mint:
chutney, roasted leg of lamb with mint-flavored
potatoes and, 101–2
-ginger sauce, crisp purses with shrimp, scallops
and, 38–39
mousse, fennel and cauliflower, squash blossoms
with, 178–79
Mrs. Ayyer's vegetable *biryani* with tempered
onion-cucumber *raita*, 170–71
mung bean:
dumplings with tomato *raita*, 181–82

power chocolate soufflé, 186–87

Provençal herb(s):

cassoulet of veal with tempered lentils and, 97

-seared salmon with sweet carrot confit, 142–43

pudding, coconut rice, 202–3

quail:

oven-roasted, with tandoori-honey emulsion and quinoa with almond sprouts and baby bok choy, 127–28

tea-smoked, with Hyderabad biryani, 124–26

quinoa with almond sprouts, oven-roasted quail with tandoori-honey emulsion, baby bok choy and, 127–28

ragout, spicy lentil, Cornish game hens with, 116–18

raita:

tempered onion-cucumber, Mrs. Ayyer's vegetable biryani with, 170–71

tomato, mung bean dumplings with, 181–82

raspberry sauce, crab crustillant with, 36–37

ratatouille, Indian spiced, 81–82

red snapper with garlic, cumin, and purple potatoes, 163–65

red wine, pepper-spiced figs in, 191

rice, *see* basmati rice; *biryani*

risotto, basmati-truffle, supreme of pheasant with, 132–32

roasted leg of lamb with mint chutney and mint-flavored potatoes, 101–2

roulade of tuna tartare with unfiltered sesame oil and brunois of green mango, 28–29

saffron, 13

-carrot soup, 56–57

-mango soup, chilled, 207

potato gratin with onions, garlic and, 83

salads, 62–76

carpaccio of cured beef with baby greens and mung bean polenta, 64–66

corn compote in a pappadam bowl, 74–76

crostini of salmon with lemon-leek sauce, 70–71

lobster tail with red and yellow pepper coulis and potato roulade, 67–69

pan-seared scallops with garlic-scented zucchini, 72–73

salmon:

crostini of, with lemon-leek sauce, 70–71

fillet of, with dill and turmeric emulsion, 144–45

Provençal herb-seared, with sweet carrot confit, 142–43

salsa, mango-papaya, opakapaka with, 151–52

sandalwood chips, poussins smoked on, with Israeli couscous, 120–21

sauces:

blending of, 19

caramelized curry, duck breasts with confit of sweet potatoes and, 129–30

curried blackberry, baby lamb racks with curry leaf-black pepper crust and, 103–5

curried blueberry, tenderloin of pork with black mustard rub, collard greens and, 88–89

dark chocolate, anise-flavored chocolate meringues with, 188–90

lemon-leek, crostini of salmon with, 70–71

mango-jalapeño, grouper with, 153–54

mint-ginger, crisp purses with shrimp, scallops and, 38–39

raspberry, crab crustillant with, 36–37

warm bittersweet chocolate, 186–87

Sauternes wine, in fresh fruit with herb-infused syrup, 195

savory spinach gratin, 78–79

scallops:

crisp purses with shrimp, mint-ginger sauce and, 38–39

lemon-cilantro ceviche of, 33

pan-seared, with garlic scented zucchini, 72–73

sea bass, fillet of, with Madras curry masala, 161–62

seafood, *see* fish; specific seafoods

seaweed tamarind rolls, spice-crusted tuna with, 155–57